THE
CLEAR
PATH

THE
CLEAR
PATH

A GUIDE TO WRITING ENGLISH ESSAYS

CONSTANCE ROOKE
University of Guelph

Nelson Canada

I(T)P   An International Thomson Publishing Company

Toronto • Albany • Bonn • Boston • Cincinnati • Detroit • London • Madrid • Melbourne
Mexico City • New York • Pacific Grove • Paris • San Francisco • Singapore • Tokyo • Washington

I(T)P ™
International Thomson Publishing
The ITP logo is a trademark under licence

Published in 1995 by
Nelson Canada
A division of Thomson Canada Limited
1120 Birchmount Road, Scarborough, Ontario M1K 5G4

Cover art: *Prairie Road* (1925), by Charles F. Comfort. Hart House Permanent Collection, University of Toronto
Cover design and interior design: Kevin Connolly

Canadian Cataloguing in Publication Data
Rooke, Constance, date

    The clear path : a guide to writing English essays
ISBN 0-17-604831-6

1. English language – Rhetoric.   2. Criticism –
Authorship.   3. Report writing.   I. Title.

PE1479.C7R66 1995   808'. 0668   C94–932357–8

Acquisitions Editor	Andrew Livingston
Production Editor	Bob Kohlmeier
Developmental Editor	Joanne Scattolon
Art Director	Liz Harasymczuk
Senior Production Coordinator	Sheryl Emery
Senior Composition Analyst	Alicja Jamorski
Input Operator	Elaine Andrews

Printed and bound in Canada
1 2 3 4 (WC) 99 98 97 96

CONTENTS

PREFACE

Writing well is a skill, just like skiing well or playing the saxophone well. It takes work to learn the rules, to refine one's technique, and to develop real power and panache. Much of this work is lonely and hard—an uphill path, in fact. The purpose of this book is to make your path as clear and easy as possible. Because I've spent a fair bit of time on this path myself, and have accompanied others along the way, I think I know a good many of the pitfalls you're likely to encounter. I also know the rules, and a few useful tricks.

This book starts with a discussion of how to generate ideas for a literary essay, how to create a thesis, how to organize those ideas, and how to improve your style. Then I take you on an arduous journey through four versions of a student essay. I begin with a failing paper on Eudora Welty's story "A Worn Path" (which is reprinted here for your convenience); I try to explain the paper's weaknesses, and then very gradually I turn it into an essay to which I would happily give an A+. Next, I take a look at P.K. Page's poem "Cook's Mountains" and how to approach the task of explicating a poem.

The second half of the book is more technical. It includes detailed information on how to handle quotations and documentation in an English essay, and a quick guide to the rules of grammar and punctuation. It finishes up with a glossary of words that are commonly misused in student work.

Good luck! Writing well *is* difficult. But you can do this, you know. You really can.

ACKNOWLEDGMENTS

I am grateful for the suggestions and comments on the manuscript that were provided by a number of my peers from across Canada, among them Robert Calder, University of Saskatchewan; J. Douglas Kneale, University of Western Ontario; Margaret Procter, University of Toronto; and A.T. Seaman, St. Mary's University. I also wish to thank Esta Spalding and Judy Barton of the University of Guelph for their invaluable assistance in the preparation of the manuscript.

Constance Rooke

ADVICE ON
ESSAY WRITING

CHOOSING A TOPIC

Assuming that your goal is to write an excellent essay (one that has a chance of earning an A grade), and that you are making up your own topic, I would recommend that you build an essay around some exciting idea (or set of ideas) you have had *or* (if you haven't had any exciting ideas yet) something that is bothering you about the text. Either of these approaches can lead to a first-class essay. Either should mean that you are *interested* in the task at hand—and that is surely the crucial point. What you want to avoid is a topic that does not challenge you, or one that is unlikely to take you into rewarding areas of investigation.

Particularly if you choose something that is bothering you, something you still haven't figured out, you may find that it doesn't work out. If you find yourself floundering, ask yourself whether this is a good time to *abandon ship* and switch over to another topic. It's often a good idea to try out more than one topic for an essay. This may seem like a waste of time, but it isn't if your goal is to find something really good.

If you are choosing from a list of assigned topics, again you should look for something that challenges you to think for yourself. The main thing to avoid is a topic that you know will just mean rehashing ideas you have picked up in class.

Generally, you should avoid topics that are too big or that will lead you too far away from the text. Remember that the success of your essay will depend to a large extent on the intelligent analysis of *detail* in the text.

You may be reluctant to choose a small (narrowly defined) topic because you fear that it will not give you an opportunity to get into the heart of the text. Usually, that fear is mistaken. Since elements of a literary text are interrelated, almost any small topic will allow you to get into the big questions. In fact, this is often a problem: you choose one small thread and keep pulling, and find that the whole fabric of the text is on the table. Instead of finding that you don't have *enough* to say, you may discover that you have too much, and that you don't know how to organize it all in a manageable structure. But at least the choice of a supposedly small topic will help you to *enter the text* with some degree of specificity.

To *try out* a topic, go back to the text and see if you can find the textual evidence for an interesting argument. Remember that you don't want to use just the detail that has been discussed in class, unless you can use it in a new way. If you don't find anything, try another topic.

When you are working with an assigned topic, or choosing from a list of assigned topics, you should keep in mind several things. In most cases the topic does not give you the thesis; that is, it does not state a position. Topics often begin with words like "examine" or "consider." Such words do not mean that you should wander around in a topic; they are a polite way of asking you to articulate an *opinion* about something, and to demonstrate the validity of that opinion by using logic and evidence. To "discuss" effectively you must decide *what it is you are going to show* and fit it together under a thesis. Sometimes the topic simply identifies a general area of investigation, like the "setting" of a story. Sometimes it asks you explicitly to take a stand on some question, such as whether race is an important issue in the story "A Worn Path." However the topic is posed, it is your responsibility to find something *interesting* in it and to develop a worthwhile thesis.

CREATING A THESIS

Once you have selected a topic, you must narrow it down and find a workable *thesis*. The thesis is the argument; it is your opinion about some aspect of the text. But this opinion cannot be plucked out of the air, or adapted from your own repertoire of opinions and then imposed upon the text. A good thesis—that is to say, a sustainable argument—must be consistent with the details of the text, which you will go on to analyze in the body of the essay. As you did in selecting a topic, choose a thesis that is small enough (focused and particular enough) to invite that detailed level of analysis.

Remember that a good thesis is not self-evident; it is debatable, inspiring you to rise to its defence. If your essay just states the obvious, it will not be interesting; your reader will wonder why you bothered to write it in the first place.

Take note: Many English teachers *require* students to include a thesis statement in the introduction of the essay. Sometimes teachers ask students to submit a thesis statement before submitting the essay itself, so that they can see whether you have embarked on a sensible path. The thesis statement is simply a condensed statement of the argument—your essay's *big idea*. Whether or not your teacher explicitly requires a thesis statement, it's always a good idea to try to state your thesis in one sentence before you begin to write the essay itself. It may turn out to be just the sentence you want for the end of the first paragraph! But even if this version of the thesis statement does not survive, it will help you to see for yourself whether you've got an appropriately focused and unified idea.

To show you the differences between a weak thesis and a strong one, I will take a terrible thesis statement, explain its weaknesses, and move it through a couple of revisions.

Topic: Discuss Phoenix's relationship to nature in "A Worn Path."

Thesis 1:   In "A Worn Path," Phoenix has a good relationship with nature.

The problem here is that the word "good" is vague. What does it mean to have a good relationship with nature? The answer to that question needs to be part of the thesis.

Thesis 2:   In "A Worn Path," Phoenix treats nature with respect.

This thesis is stronger than the previous one because it identifies what is meant by "good." But the thesis still doesn't explain why Phoenix treats nature with respect. Furthermore, because this respect for nature is obvious in the text, the thesis is neither interesting nor debatable.

Thesis 3:   In "A Worn Path," Phoenix treats nature with respect because she sees it as God's creation.

This gets at the reason for Phoenix's respect for nature. It draws a connection between her response to nature and her spirituality, which takes us into the heart of the story. Most importantly, the thesis can be supported by interesting *details*—references to nature that have a spiritual quality (e.g., the bird that flies by and is associated with "God watching me the whole time").

There are many possible thesis statements for every topic. Here are some examples of thesis statements I've created for a single topic.

Topic: Examine Silas's relationship with the alligator in *Crawl*.

Thesis 1:   In *Crawl*, Silas treats the alligator as an ally in his battle against the adult world.

Thesis 2:   In *Crawl,* the alligator represents the realm of childhood fantasy, which, at the end of the novel, Silas realizes he must leave behind.

Thesis 3:   The alligator, because it lives in the sewer and appears in Silas's nightmares, represents the protagonist's deepest fears.

BEING A TEACHER/LAWYER

Just as we want a literary work to do something to us, to change how we see things, so a really good essay about literature should surprise the reader. Think of yourself as a teacher: your job is to teach the teacher. In this context, you can surprise and instruct the reader (your instructor) by convincing her (or him) of the merits of ideas she hasn't had herself, or by providing new support for familiar ideas. Say that in fact you don't come up with an idea the instructor hasn't thought of, or evidence she hasn't seen; you can still surprise her if you don't just repeat or rehash what has been said in class. One of the fatal mistakes students make is to assume that a rehash is what their teachers really want.

Notice that I said the *merits* of the idea; the instructor's job is to determine whether you've made a good case (not the only possible case). Think of yourself as a defence lawyer arguing a case to a jury. Just as the lawyer doesn't have to prove *absolutely* the innocence of the client, so you are not obliged to prove the undeniable truth of your thesis. The lawyer's job is to prove that the client could be innocent, that the scenario offered to the jury by the defence could quite easily be correct. (Notice that this involves disposing of any possibly damning evidence on the other side.) This analogy is a bit problematic, however, since you should believe in your thesis. You haven't been landed with it, after all (as a lawyer might be landed with a client); you have *chosen* this thesis because you think it is worth defending. Therefore, avoid taking on a bizarre, wildly improbable case just for the hell of it. (You want to be original; you do not want to be crazy.) Ideally, you want to be the kind of lawyer who believes passionately in a client who is not *obviously* innocent; and you want to convince the jury that your defence is sound, so that you win the case.

GETTING THE IDEAS

There is no one way, of course, but I'll tell you how I often do it. I catch wind of a possible idea, and then I mark up my text to track it down. I notice something—say, that there is something interesting going on with birds in a text, or that the narration switches between present and future tense to good effect but for no immediately apparent reason, or that every now and again I am offended by a seemingly admirable character's behaviour or manner of speech—and I start marking each occurrence of the thing I'm interested in. I might have several things like that going. Sometimes I jot down questions and possible answers in the margin as I go along; sometimes I take notes elsewhere, using a separate page for each thing I'm pursuing. Then I go back and look at my notes and everything I've marked in the text to see if I can make anything of it. Perhaps the germ of an idea will occur to me only when I have finished reading, in which case I'll go back as soon as possible (while the germ is still active) to mark up the text and check it out.

I make more notes, getting down fast whatever occurs to me, without censoring myself too much. (I call this stage *brainstorming*.) Then I get critical. Does this make *sense?* What of all this is good, and what must I discard because it is almost certainly rubbish? Can I shape a worthwhile thesis out of what is left? What fits together? What ideas are so intriguing to me that— even though they don't obviously fit my thesis—I will try to work them in? (Sometimes in the act of writing a perfect opportunity will miraculously appear, so that it turns out the idea *does* fit after all.)

At this point, I usually write down a preliminary thesis statement (what it is I'm trying to prove). My next step is to ask myself whether I've gathered enough evidence. If not, it's back to the text. I also try to look really hard once more at each passage I think I might use, to see if there is something in it that I might have missed. This approach *often* pays off, providing me with the most interesting points in my argument.

In pushing harder for ideas, I rely heavily on the question *why* to prod me. I ask myself *why* the writer put this scene next to that one, *why* I respond a certain way, *why* this language is so formal or so flat, *why* this or that detail has been included, and so on. Whenever I come up with an idea, I try to resist breathing a sigh of relief or patting myself on the back. Instead, I try to push the idea, to keep on thinking about it. I mention this because in my experience the worst mistake students make is to quit thinking too soon; there is a tendency to give up when you think you might have rounded up enough material to fill up the pages assigned.

Another mistake that students make quite often is to get so hooked on an exciting, original idea that they refuse to let it go, even when the opposing evidence mounts and the interpretation really cannot be sustained. We all take pleasure in making discoveries on our own, and it is sometimes very hard to let that exhilaration go. But if you're wrong you have to let go! There is a fine but crucial line between not pushing far enough and pushing too far, or imposing your own ideas on the text and ignoring urgent, contradictory signals. How do you know when you've gone too far? Ask yourself as honestly as you can whether this *feels* right. Is it consistent with or does it contradict an interpretation that is obviously valid? Does it limit too far the appeal of the text's meaning?

Once you have followed all of the trails that you think are interesting and that have led in fruitful directions, you need to start thinking about what your thesis will be. Sometimes the paths you have followed will seem to converge around a *big idea*—an overriding question that has been posed and answered in the course of all your brainstorming and questioning and re-reading. Once this idea begins to take shape, you will see that some of the lines of inquiry you have pursued are off the track—and you can let those go. Now the question is how to organize what remains. To help you make your essay as effective as possible, I give advice in the next section on how to organize ideas within the body of your essay.

ORGANIZING THE IDEAS

In this section I discuss ways to organize ideas into paragraphs, as well as the organization of ideas within paragraphs. I recommend that you try using a paragraph outline—essentially a plan for an argument. A big part of the job here is to figure out what goes with what. Remember that each paragraph represents a *phase* of your argument; each is a part of what you need to accomplish in order to prove your thesis. Each phase should be distinct; thus, each paragraph should have its own *topic* to which every sentence relates.

Think of prospective paragraphs as *files;* the task at this point is to sort the ideas and the evidence into the appropriate files, and to be sure that nothing is misfiled or left out in the cold. (If I've got some especially appealing idea that doesn't seem to fit anywhere, I jot it down in the margin—so that I'll remember it in case it turns out that I can use it after all.) Later, each file will become a paragraph. If the file gets too bulky, it will eventually have to be broken down into two or more paragraphs. If it is too skimpy, it will have to be combined with another in some logical way. So try to be sure now that each file is of a manageable size.

What is a manageable size? How long should a paragraph be? Half of a typed page is an average length for a paragraph. You will want to vary the length of paragraphs, but avoid too many short paragraphs and try not to have a page on which there is no paragraph break at all. Very short paragraphs typically occur when you fail to develop ideas or to combine related ideas. Very long paragraphs are hard on the reader, and can usually be avoided.

At this stage, you should also try to discover the best possible order for the paragraphs. Sometimes this is easy; sometimes it's hard. Remember that your paragraphs are *stages in an argument* or a lesson. You need to figure out what things the reader needs to be shown prior to being shown something else; an essay is a developmental learning curve that you control. You need to think about logical progression. Remember that you are trying to keep the reader with you on a clearly marked trail; the reader must trust that you know where you are going, and that your moves make sense.

You might also try thinking of your essay as theatre, which typically begins with exposition (setting up the situation), continues through various developments and complications, and ends with a dramatic climax and resolution. The point here is that you want to keep the reader interested. The theatrical model of essay-writing suggests that each act should be stronger and more compelling than the one before. One trouble with this model is the requirement that you state your thesis at the beginning of the paper. Is this like telling who did it in the opening scene of a mystery? If so, go ahead and do it anyway! There can still be some element of surprise in the way you manage the ending, and you can still choose to save your most satisfying examples for the end.

You want to achieve order *within* each paragraph as well. Again, proceed in a *logical* manner (moving from A to B to C) through the phases of an idea. It may be possible to proceed in a *dramatic* manner as well, leaving the most important or surprising point for the end. But if you have to choose between logic and drama, go for logic.

In some circumstances another kind of order will suggest itself strongly—chronological order, for instance. But do spend some time *thinking* about the order of material within paragraphs and the order of the paragraphs themselves. Do this thinking at the outline stage, and do it again once you have written a draft of the essay.

Paragraph outlines can begin just as clusters of related ideas that you think might take shape as paragraphs. Eventually, though, you will probably want to have something that looks like an outline—with the paragraphs themselves in an effective order, under headings to indicate the topic of each paragraph, and the points and the evidence you intend to use for each paragraph briefly indicated (again in a likely order) under each paragraph heading. This skeleton helps you to see the bones of the essay. It helps you to see the transitions that will be needed as you move from one phase of the argument to the next.

A few of you, however, may find that to begin with an outline is counterproductive. For some people, at least on some occasions, an outline seems to make the ideas go dead on the page. When they get to the writing stage, the life is gone. You will have to experiment to see what is best for you; when you get stuck one way, you can try another. Sometimes you can just start writing, with very little idea of where you are going, and find ideas through something like free fall. *Warning*: You may want to try this method, but you shouldn't trust it. You should always stand back afterward and examine what you have written very carefully. If it has not, by some special dispensation of the gods, come out in a perfect order, *now* is the time to make an outline. Treat what you have written as raw material; keep the relevant good bits, and toss out the junk. But be sure that whatever you are tempted to turn in to your instructor looks like something that has a *solid outline beneath the flesh*; if it doesn't (and it probably won't) don't stop. Make that outline now, and adjust the text to fit it. Do not quit because you have come up with the requisite number of words.

Even when you are working from a very detailed outline, you will find that *as you write* new (and sometimes better) ideas occur to you. Sentences will appear on your page that suggest new possibilities for development and new connections. This is a major part of the pleasure of writing. Don't be afraid to take advantage of insights that arrive in this way. Just be sure that you make the necessary adjustments to your essay plan, so that the structure of your essay is clear. (I find that I almost always make some adjustments in my paragraph outline when I get down to the job of writing.)

How do I know how to organize the ideas I have? In the next section, I suggest two possible ways of organizing ideas on *The Last Savages* (a novel I have invented for the sake of this example).

Topic: Examine the depiction of Native people in William Smith's *The Last Savages.*

Thesis: Basing his assumptions about culture on a white, Western European model, William Smith in *The Last Savages* reinforces negative stereotypes of Native people.

Now consider the pieces of this thesis.

1. The book contains stereotypes of Native people.
2. The stereotypes are negative.
3. The stereotypes follow from Smith's white, Western European view of the world.

Let's assume that Smith relies on five basic stereotypes about Native people. The question then is how to order the five stereotypes. In a good essay, the order would not be simply random. It might, for example, be the case that some of the stereotypes *seem* positive while others are obviously negative. Remember that part of what you are arguing in this essay is that the stereotypes are negative. You could use your introduction to discuss the sense in which all stereotypes have damaging consequences, though some appear to be complimentary. In this case, you might move from the apparently positive to the most obviously negative—or the other way around. Either way, you are dealing with the issue of *negative* stereotypes at the same time that you are moving through the examples.

Another way of organizing this paper might be to assign a paragraph to each of Smith's cultural assumptions, and to fit the stereotypes that follow from those assumptions into those paragraphs.

TWO COMMON MODES OF ORGANIZATION

In this section, I want to say a few words about two modes of organization that are often appropriate for an English essay: organization by *classification* and by *comparison/contrast*. One or another of these may make obvious sense as the basic organizational mode for a particular essay. The choice of one of these basic organizational modes does not preclude the internal use of the other. Thus, you may need to use comparisons in a classification essay, or to classify items in a comparison/contrast essay.

Classification

In literary criticism, classification—putting items into categories—is often a valuable tool. For example, you might classify something as a tragedy, or as a romance, or as a feminist text. You might classify a character as heroic. These terms, which refer to literary tradition, can illuminate aspects of the particular text at hand *and* show how literary texts grow out of similar preoccupations and conventions. In this style of classification, you would first define your term (tragedy, for example) and then, using textual evidence, show why the text you are analyzing belongs in this category. This might be an interesting thing to do if the text in question is not obviously a tragedy.

Another useful kind of classification essay seeks to classify items from the text into different categories. For example, you might classify the kinds of imagery in a text. When you are using classification, always keep your purpose in mind. What do you *learn* about the text by putting textual items into categories? Say you are looking at the kinds of humour used in a text. What do these uses reveal about the characters? What do they reveal about the themes of the text? Classification can be an important tool for revealing patterns within a text. And that's one of the main things that literary criticism is about: rising above the trees to see the forest, and to see how carefully the paths are laid out.

Suppose you notice that the character Morgan is strangely silent during many of the scenes in the novel *Twelve Angry Women* (another text I have invented!). You might begin to take notes classifying *according to the reasons for her silence* all those occasions on which Morgan is silent. You discover that she is silent for one of three reasons: she is angry, or guilty, or afraid. You observe that each of these types of silence seems to be accompanied by a particular gesture or behaviour. For instance, when Morgan is silent and afraid she wrings her hands. You decide that a discussion of the three kinds of silence would make an interesting essay. This is probably not yet reason enough to write the essay. *So what* if there are three different kinds of silence with three different accompanying gestures? Why is this an important discovery? It may be—but always ask yourself this question. Say that in looking for these different kinds of silence, you reread the final courtroom scene—and find that you have to read it in a new way! Morgan's silence in the court has been interpreted by your teacher and classmates (or by some famous critic) as evidence of her guilt. You notice, however, that her gesture in this scene is not the one that signifies guilt. You can reinterpret the final scene in a convincing way; the *evidence* you have assembled shows that Morgan's real emotion here is fear.

Thesis: Morgan is not guilty: she remains silent in the final courtroom scene because she is afraid.

Paragraph 1 (introduction): Give the usual interpretation of the ending. Disagree and state thesis. Point out that she is often silent—when angry, guilty, or afraid—and that specific gestures associated with these silences signal to the reader the reason for her silence in any given case. (Don't tell what the gestures are yet—I want to surprise my reader!—but end the paragraph with the idea that Morgan's gesture in the final scene proves she's innocent.)

Paragraph 2: Morgan's silence when she is angry. Three examples, moving from the one in which she is obviously furious to the one in which her anger is least clear; in each case she fiddles with her ears.

Paragraph 3: Morgan's silence when she is feeling guilty. Four clear examples. Each time she fans herself, as if shooing away a mosquito.

Paragraph 4: Morgan's silence when she is afraid. Two examples; each time she's wringing her hands. (Don't use the courtroom scene yet.)

Paragraph 5 (conclusion): The final courtroom scene. Again challenge the interpretation that Morgan is guilty. She is wringing her hands; she is not fanning herself.

Comparison/Contrast

This mode of organization allows you to show how two items (themes, characters, images, outcomes, scenes, etc.) are alike and/or different from each other. Sometimes the thrust of your paper will be to show how alike the items are, and sometimes the point will be how dissimilar they are. But a likeness is *interesting* only if it surprises us; thus, you will be pointing out that despite obvious differences (contrasts), A and B are, with respect to X, surprisingly alike (comparison). In the same way, a difference (contrast) is interesting only if we might have thought that A and B are very much alike (comparison). Keep in mind that there has to be a *reason* for comparing the two items: some illumination of the text that occurs as a result.

There are two obvious models for a comparison/contrast essay. Say you're comparing two texts, and your discussion involves nine points of comparison. One way of organizing the essay is to discuss text A first, going through all nine features; then you move on to text B, discussing the same nine features in the same order. The danger of this approach is that the essay falls into two very separate halves. To reduce the risk, be sure to refer frequently to text A in your discussion of text B, and use the introduction to establish some good reason for thinking of these two texts together.

The second obvious model for a comparison/contrast essay involves moving through the *features* (the nine points of comparison) one by one. Each feature gets a paragraph of its own, in which both texts are discussed. The danger of this approach is that you will be moving back and forth between texts so rapidly that the essay may feel both choppy and incoherent.

To solve these problems, a paper will often mix models one and two. You might do this by taking the nine features and sorting them into three categories. That way, you can discuss category 1 (including three related features) as these appear in text A and then in text B; then category 2 (involving three related features) for text A and then text B; and finally category 3 (involving three related features) for text A and then text B. It won't always be as tidy as this, but I hope you get the idea!

Now for more imaginary texts that I will use to suggest a means of organizing ideas for a comparison/contrast essay.

Topic: Compare and contrast images of the sea in "The Gale" and "Under Polaris."

Thesis: Both stories draw upon literary archetypes of the sea in ways that intensify reader response.

Introduction: Introduce the three archetypes: the sea as creator/destroyer, as testing ground for the hero, and as an arena for change. (Mention

Shakespeare's *The Tempest*—say it's alluded to in both stories: "There is nothing but doth suffer a sea-change into something rich and strange.") State thesis.

Paragraph 1: Creator/destroyer. In "Under Polaris," while sailing alone across the Atlantic, Eliza falls into the sea. Though terrified, she floats: "The sea carried her like a mother." Later she loses the main mast in a storm and nearly loses the ship.

Paragraph 2: Creator/destroyer. In "The Gale," the captain's son has his first swimming lesson off the bowsprit. Compare the childish joy of the son to Eliza's joy upon floating. Later the son is killed in the storm.

Paragraph 3: Testing ground for hero. In both stories, the heroes are tested by the storm. Eliza faces "the challenge that would determine whether she could ever believe in herself again." The storm in "The Gale" shows the captain his "mortality." He is compared to Ulysses.

Paragraph 4: Arena of change. Both texts allude to the final scenes of *The Tempest* where Prospero's right to the Dukedom of Milan is asserted. Like Prospero, Eliza wins the championship sailing title that was stolen from her. The captain regains the respect of his crew. These victories may not seem like allusions to *The Tempest,* but given the odd references to pearls in both stories (compare Shakespeare's "These are pearls that were his eyes") as well as more obvious allusions to *The Tempest,* they probably are.

Conclusion: The references to *The Tempest* and Ulysses, as well as the three associated archetypes of the sea, make the reader aware of an ancient tradition to which these contemporary stories belong. At the same time, we recognize with a deep sense of satisfaction the departure from tradition (a "sea-change"!) these stories represent: thus Eliza, a young woman, can be an archetypal hero.

INTRODUCTION

The introduction (usually the first paragraph of the essay) is very important. Some writers feel that they cannot go on until they get the introduction exactly right; others hurry through it in a first draft because they have learned from experience that what they actually write in the body of the essay will often require significant changes in the introduction by the time they're done. In either case—whether you have slaved over the introduction or not—you should *always* go back at the end to see whether the introduction (and in particular the thesis statement) still works.

You may have been taught the "funnel" model for an introduction. This involves starting off with something broad and funnelling down to the narrowly defined thesis of your essay at the end of the paragraph. Funnelling, or zeroing in on the topic in the introduction, often works extremely well. But it is not the only possible model, and not always the best.

Students often get the *tone* of an introduction wrong. You should avoid being stuffy or pretentious, and you should not waste time offering compliments to the author. An introduction should not contain puffery or *filler*. You cannot afford to waste time with filler anywhere in the essay, but I mention this here because introductions are often guilty of this crime—especially at the broad part of the funnel. Whatever the broad portion of the funnel contains (assuming that you employ this useful model), remember that it has to *count*; it should be necessary to the argument that follows.

The introduction should give your reader some idea of where the paper is going, what its thesis is, and perhaps how you are going to proceed—but don't feel that you have to give away all your secrets at the start. In a short essay, the introduction usually takes just one paragraph. In a longer essay, the introduction is often longer, and the first *paragraph* is sometimes used to provide a kind of background to the argument, so that the thesis appears a bit later.

In a short and relatively uncomplicated essay, you should be wary of using the introduction to tell the reader exactly what you are going to say in the body of the essay and in what order. (Avoid "First I will show X; then I will show Y; finally I will show Z.") This leads to unnecessary repetition and a dull essay. Often, in a good short essay, the introduction indicates the stages of the argument more subtly. For example, the introduction might say that "The author accomplishes this through X, Y, and Z," and the body of the essay is then committed to dealing with X, Y, and Z *in that order.*

Incidentally, it may be perfectly all right to use the first person ("I") in an English essay, but you should do so only for a good reason. Ask your instructor if you are uncertain. (A good reason might be that you are tracking the stages of your own response or the reasons for that response.)

Every essay must have a thesis. Usually, the thesis is contained in a sentence or two near the end of the introduction. (This portion of the introduction is called the *thesis statement.*) Be sure that you understand the difference between a topic and a thesis. The topic is what the essay is about (setting, let's say); the thesis is what you are trying to *prove* about the topic (for example, that the physical setting of a certain story establishes a mood of stagnation, which is critical to the reader's understanding of the main character).

Using the thesis about setting that I have proposed, the body of the essay might go on to present and *analyze* (probably in chronological order) carefully selected examples of stagnation—a swamp, mould growing on things in a refrigerator, etc.—and to connect these with the growth of the reader's awareness of a comparable stagnation in the life of the protagonist.

The introduction itself might look something like this:

> Alex Sutherland, the narrator of "In the Swamp," clearly thinks he is a man of purpose, a man on the go. His constant activity and frequent praise of his own energy may convince an unwary reader that this is so. However, details of the physical setting confirm the message of the title, that Alex is stuck in a kind of swamp. These images of stagnation should help the reader to understand that Alex is not the man he thinks he is.

This introduction does not seem to follow the funnel model, but in a way it does. The student moves from something that may seem evident in a hasty, broad view of the story to something more subtle and particular (the images of stagnation, which provide the thesis of the essay). Using a more obvious funnel, the student might have begun like this: "A wary reader should always be alert to the possibility that the narrator is deceiving us, or that he deceives himself. Alex Sutherland . . .," etc. Now the lip of the funnel extends beyond the limits of this particular story, to make a general claim. But either of these two versions is fine.

THE BODY OF THE ESSAY

Avoid plot summary. The essay should make some sense even to someone who doesn't know the text you are discussing, but don't waste time retelling the plot. The trick here is to orient your reader to the action while *at the same time* proceeding with your argument. This is one of the hardest things for students to learn. And excessive plot summary is one of the most common—and fatal—shortcomings of student essays. Check to see that you are not wasting time in this way. To put the matter bluntly, a sentence that merely tells the story contributes nothing to the merit of the essay or to the grade you receive.

Here's an example of a paragraph that is almost entirely plot summary. Be *very* careful not to fall into this trap.

> Alex is just stagnating. Flora isn't interested in him, and he just won't give up. He goes to her house, he rings the bell, he is carrying chocolates

and flowers, and he is wearing those silly plaid pants left over from grade eight. Flora tries to shut the door on him, but he falls down "weeping at her feet" (83). "He grabs her ankles, he cries, he pleads" (84). Alex can't understand that she doesn't like him. She threatens to call the police, but he still can't get the message.

Use present tense. In general, when you refer to the present time of the text, use the *present* tense: "Alex Sutherland, the narrator of 'In the Swamp,' *thinks* he *is* a man of purpose" (*not* "thought he was"). This is the basic tense, from which you depart as the need arises: "As a child, Alex had feared that he would die young; now he fears that he will not."

Analyze evidence. Don't fill your essay up with quotations on which you offer no comment. Before or after the quotation, *analyze* it—or at least be sure that the *point* of the quotation (how *you* are using it) is clear to the reader. Remember that the reader cannot read your mind.

Select examples carefully. In most cases, there will be more evidence than you can use. Don't feel that you have to give it all. Choose the most persuasive as well as the most subtle and interesting examples. Although you should not be afraid of using important examples cited in class, you should always try to find fresh examples of your own. Avoid using too many examples that make exactly the same point.

Control the flow. Check for paragraph unity. Each paragraph should have a general topic, and everything in the paragraph should relate to that topic. Be sure that your reader remains aware of what the topic is, but don't beat him over the head with it. Each sentence should lead into the next in an easy and logical manner. Place signposts along the trail, so that the reader can keep track of your argument (and can be confident that *you* are on track). If you change direction, provide a signal to that effect—a word such as "however"; if you want to be sure that the reader knows that the next bit follows from the last, consider a word like "thus" or "therefore," but don't become excessively reliant on such devices. Your reader shouldn't feel that you are being too stiff or too bossy, or that you think he hasn't got a brain in his head. Be sure too that you have achieved an effective or natural transition as you move from one paragraph to the next. Remember that you want to keep the reader with you every step of the way. The reader should not be frustrated and confused *or* irritated and bored. The reader's journey through the words of your essay is *in your hands,* the hands that have written the words. Remember that the reader can read only the words on the page. *The reader cannot read your mind.*

CONCLUSION

In a short essay, the conclusion should avoid an extensive repetition of points already made. A good conclusion may remind us of those points, however. Often it returns to the thesis (of which we should *always* be reminded at the end) in a slightly different way. A good conclusion often goes beyond what was said in the body of the paper, to assess the larger implications of the thesis.

Students are sometimes told that the argument should be completed prior to the conclusion, and that new evidence and new ideas should not appear in the conclusion. That advice seems to me just a bit suspect, especially for a short essay. Certainly you want to have completed the basic argument before you get to the conclusion. Your case should be secure before that point. But you might still pull a rabbit or two out of the magician's hat in the last paragraph.

A good conclusion provides *the sense of an ending*. Have you ever been to a play and been unsure whether it's time to clap? That uncertainty in the reader is what you want to avoid. In a very short essay, you may have so much to pack into a few paragraphs that you cannot afford to have a final paragraph that is bereft of new ideas. In that case, just be sure that the last paragraph reminds the reader of the thesis and that it provides the sense of an ending.

REMARKS ON STYLE

In talking about how to write a good essay, I have used the analogy of a path or a trail. One of the main things you *don't* want on a trail is *deadwood*. This obscures the trail and slows your reader down. What do I mean by the term *deadwood*? I mean words that are dead because they serve no function; they just take up space. I mean *wordiness*, which is one of the most common and deplorable characteristics of bad writing.

There are two principal (and often overlapping) types of wordiness. In one kind, the words just take up space, trying to sound impressive and failing to say anything—perhaps even for a full paragraph, or a full essay. Usually you know when you're doing this; this kind of bad writing is often a handy but ill-advised substitute for the hard job of *thinking*. The sentences may sound all right, but there's nothing at all behind them; the words are just puffed up with hot air. In the second kind of wordiness, there is meaning in there somewhere. But the live wood—the real structure of thought—is obscured by the deadwood, the *useless words* that the writer may have stuck in out of a mistaken sense that they sound good. Sometimes, students are afraid their ideas sound too simple, so they haul in the deadwood. (Wordiness is a disease that has also—and unpleasantly but aptly—been likened to diarrhea.)

Many common expressions are wordy and should be avoided. The meaning they contain can be expressed much more concisely. Thus, for example, "on account of the fact that" really means "because"; "at this point in time" really means "now"; and "in spite of the fact that" really means "although."

Getting rid of wordiness can mean choosing exact nouns, verbs, adjectives, and adverbs (not "She ran as quickly as she could down the street" but "She sprinted down the street"); replacing inexact adverbs (such as "really," "rather," "somewhat," "very") with a more precise word (not "really happy" but "ecstatic"); eliminating redundancies (not "cooperating together" but "cooperating"; not "the two twins" but "the twins"); and condensing phrases to single words (not "in the event that" but "if").

I'm going to take a sentence through several versions now, clearing away the deadwood:

1. Because of the work he did in the 1940s and 1950s, Humphrey Bogart could, by some, be considered legendary in terms of his film career.
2. Because of his work in the 1940s and 1950s, Humphrey Bogart is considered by some to be legendary in terms of his film career.
3. Humphrey Bogart is considered legendary in terms of his film career.
4. Humphrey Bogart is considered a film legend.
5. Humphrey Bogart is a film legend.

This sentence keeps getting stronger. Has anything been lost since the first version? Probably not, although we would have to know more about the context to establish that. But even if you do need to specify his work in the 1940s and 1950s, the first version of this sentence is very bad. You could say this instead:

Because of his work in the 1940s and 1950s, Humphrey Bogart is a film legend.

Observe that the phrase "in terms of his film career" has to go!

Don't take simple points and try to make them *sound* complicated. The true struggle is to take a complicated thought and express it in a sentence that is as simple and clear as possible. I'll give you another example now of a wordy sentence, with a revision that is much stronger:

1. One of the most disturbing types of possible tendencies that occurs when we begin the act of writing is an inability of sorts to suitably render into concise and wholly efficient language our multidimensional ranges of various ideas.

2. A major problem in writing is the inability to express our ideas concisely.

Two good things happen when you move from the first to the second version. You make the point easier to follow, *and* you take up less space, so that
now there is more room in the essay for the other things you want to say. You
should be ruthless with yourself. If a word or phrase isn't doing anything, if
you don't *need* it, get rid of it. *Be concise.*

Let's do some more. Say I have a sentence like this one:

*It could be said that the poets from the Romantic time period were inter-
ested in issues concerning our place in the natural world.*

Let's think about the opening clause, "It could be said that the poets from the
Romantic time period." What do I mean? Well, I really mean "the Romantic
poets." So that's what I should say. The sentence is now much stronger—

The Romantic poets were interested in issues concerning our place in the
natural world.

How much do we lose if the sentence is stripped down further? Does the
author really mean something more than "The Romantic poets were interested in nature"? Perhaps so . . .

Here's another:

Margaret Atwood, a Canadian writer, has thus far in her career written in
four genres: she has written novels, short stories, poetry, and criticism.

The most obvious things to take out are "thus far in her career," because that
fact is implied, and "she has written," because it is redundant. This would
leave the following:

Margaret Atwood, a Canadian writer, has written in four genres: novels,
short stories, poetry, and criticism.

Beyond that, your changes will depend on context. If for some reason you
wanted to emphasize that she is Canadian, you would keep "a Canadian
writer" in the sentence. But this is probably just filler. If you really wanted to
stress the range of her work you might get away with saying that she has
written in four genres. But it's probably more filler. If you aren't particularly
concerned about the issue of genre, then "Margaret Atwood has written
novels, short stories, poetry, and criticism" is surely sufficient.

Think about some of the filler we all use from time to time. What does "it is my opinion that" contribute to a sentence? The fact that you are making your point in the first place is evidence enough that this is what you think. Start right in with your point. You don't need to say, for example, "It is my opinion that Hamlet is an existentialist." Just say "Hamlet is an existentialist," and then go on to explain why you think so. Similarly, the expression "it can be seen that" adds nothing to the meaning of a sentence. Instead of saying "It can be seen that Thomas King is drawing upon oral tradition in *Green Grass, Running Water,*" just say "Thomas King draws upon oral tradition in *Green Grass, Running Water.*"

Sometimes wordiness is more difficult to fix. Even if there's a good idea hidden under the deadwood, it can be very hard to find. To show you what I mean, here's a sentence that demonstrates extreme wordiness.

By way of conclusion, I would like to posit that with regard to colonization and granting the fact that the negatively affecting characteristics of the colonial mentality are complex, Jean Rhys makes the point astutely.

What am I trying to say here? It's hard to say, but the sentence might mean something like this:

In her novel, Jean Rhys analyses the complexity of colonization and its overwhelmingly negative effects.

Probably the hardest part of writing is the struggle for clarity. It's also the most exciting part. You may think of this as the struggle to translate what you think into words, but often it's more than that. Often, you *find out* what you think in the struggle of writing, or you find out that what you thought isn't quite right—now that you're staring at it, naked on the page—and that you are going to have to think some more. There are two good reasons for writing: to communicate something to the *reader,* and to communicate something to *yourself.* That second reason is not as obvious or as widely understood as the first, but it is a very potent reason all the same. We clarify our own thoughts by writing well; and when we do succeed in getting those thoughts down clearly on paper, we possess them much more thoroughly than we did when they were just buzzing around inside our brains. (When we write badly, we get frustrated—because we suspect that the makings of something much better is lurking in our heads. We just can't get it *out!*)

The struggle to be concise and clear occurs at the level of the sentence. You fight to make *each sentence* as tight and as clear as possible. You may sometimes feel that these are competing claims: you think that in order to be *clear,* you will have to be less *concise* (taking more time to say what you mean). *That may well be true.* But what often happens in the writing process is that you don't quite hit on what you mean in one whack (one sentence), so you take a few more whacks (more sentences)—trying to zoom in on the point you want to make. That's O.K. for a rough draft. But in the revision process, you should step back and ask yourself whether *now* you are in a position to say this thing more quickly. Reduce the total numbers of words as far as you can without sacrificing clarity.

Be concrete. Be precise. In choosing your words, prefer the particular to the general wherever possible. Consider this sentence: "Here one sees his lack of emotion." What exactly is meant by "lack of emotion"? This *could* mean any number of things, like indifference, or iciness, or impartiality; each of these words is more particular, more precise than "lack of emotion." And any one of these, if it succeeds in capturing your idea, would be preferable to "lack of emotion," since that term gives the reader only a general idea of what you might mean. Now consider this sentence: "The clown's part in *Othello* is very small." There is nothing wrong with that sentence, but this one is better: "The clown in *Othello* speaks only thirty lines." You have still spent only eight words on the sentence, and the general idea (that the part is very small) is still there; but now the sentence is more concrete and more precise. The reader gets a bigger return on the time that was spent in reading these eight words—a more precise picture, and a piece of hard information— and loses nothing.

Choose the right word. Sometimes a *thesaurus* will help you to find exactly the right word; it will give you possible synonyms (words that mean more or less the same thing) from which to choose the word that says it best. (In fact, few words are *really* synonymous; there are usually shades of meaning that make one word more appropriate than another in a particular context.) The best word is often the most particular word. To achieve precision, you choose the word that narrows the field. Is skiing "enjoyable" or "exhilarating"? It may well be enjoyable, but so are lots of things. You want the word that scores a bull's-eye. You want the word to land in the precise location of the thing you are describing, rather than on one of the outer circles.

When you look up a word in the thesaurus, you are often given a number of possible synonyms. Some are so imprecise that you can discard them immediately, while others seem fine. Before you use any of the ones you think are fine, look up each one in the dictionary. There is no point in using a thesaurus if you are trying only to find the biggest and fanciest word you can and are not interested in the precision of your language. Often you are given a list of other words to see; it doesn't hurt to look them up as long as you follow the same procedure before you use them.

Consider level of diction. Has X been incarcerated, thrown in the slammer, or sent to prison? The first is too highfalutin or stiff, the second is too low or colloquial, and the third is fine. Don't be afraid of saying things simply. "Exhilarating" is better than "enjoyable" in the example given previously, not because it is fancier but because it is more precise. In most situations, for example, I would use the word "use" where others might (as they would say) *employ* the word "employ"—because it sounds fancier. I like "use" better because I don't see any good reason for using the fancier word. The best writers in my experience are not afraid of using striking or unusual words *or* of using good, strong, simple words. And the mix is most pleasing to most readers.

Because you will be writing formal academic essays, the level of diction is important. One of the things that determines the level you should use is your target audience. For academic essays, your target audience is your professor, so your tone should be formal and professional.

Prefer the active voice. The great advantage of the active voice—"I broke the window"—over the passive voice—" The window was broken"—is that the active voice requires you to take or assign responsibility; in the passive voice the actor of the verb is obscured. For that very reason, politicians are fond of the passive voice. Certainly, there are occasions when your meaning will require that you use the passive. These would include scientific experiments (*example:* The beaker was filled with water, and a flame was placed beneath it) and cases in which the agent of the action is understood, unimportant, or unknown (*example:* It was said at the meeting that the new development would interfere with the wildlife). If you have a choice, though, prefer the active. Writing that overuses the passive voice tends to be abstract, stuffy, and weak.

Vary sentence structure. You should provide variety both in the *length* and in the *structure* of sentences. Too many short or long sentences in a row should be avoided. A short sentence can be very effective, especially after a long one. However, more than a couple of short sentences in a row can sound choppy—and juvenile. Learn how to *combine* sentences effectively. Make effective use of introductory elements—starting with a dependent clause, a participial phrase, etc. You should be concerned if nearly all your sentences start with the subject of the main clause. Don't be afraid to use parallel construction, semicolons, and colons; it is important to learn how to use these well. Use the full range of conjunctive adverbs and conjunctions, not just a few like "but." (See pages 83 and 87–88.)

Here are some examples of ways to combine sentences:

Phoenix is an old woman. She travels the same path over and over. She must get her grandson his medicine. Her journey is a long one.

1. Though she is an old woman, Phoenix travels the same long path over and over to get the medicine for her grandson.
2. Travelling the same long path over and over, old Phoenix must get medicine for her grandson.
3. In spite of the long journey and her old age, Phoenix must travel the same path over and over to get her grandson his medicine.

Notice that the emphasis of the sentence changes with the change in openings. What was once a choppy group of sentences becomes, by combining sentences, a smooth, unified statement.

In the Quick Guide to Grammar and Punctuation is a section on clauses that lists the different types of subordinate clauses. (See pages 85–86.) These types of clauses are the building blocks for sentence combining.

Here is an example of a paragraph I can improve by combining sentences:

> Spenser's poetry reflects the attitudes of the Royal Court. Queen Elizabeth used her private life as a tool for foreign policy. Therefore, the private message of the love poems written by her court poet, Spenser, was also a tool of foreign policy. You can see this in the poems' description of the lover. The descriptions are unlike descriptions in love poems by other poets. They do not reveal the intimate self of a lover. They reveal a courtly persona.

This paragraph says a lot. But it says it inefficiently and without making adequate connections between the ideas of the sentences. Combining sentences forces you to subordinate some ideas to others; the ideas are put together in a way that suggests their relationship to one another.

> Spenser's poetry reflects Queen Elizabeth's use of her private life as a tool of foreign policy. That the private messages of the love poems are also tools of foreign policy is revealed in the descriptions of the lover, which suggest a courtly persona rather than the intimate self of a lover described by other love poets.

CHECK YOUR WORK!

This is a critical factor in the success or failure of your essay. You must leave time to check your work *very* carefully; to omit this task or to spend only a few minutes on it can be costly. Remember that your purpose here is to find out what's wrong, and what could be improved, *not* to convince yourself that the essay is fine as it stands. Two things can lull you into a false sense of security: the lovely sight of a cleanly typed page, and the flattering sound of your own voice reading the essay out loud. I strongly recommend both things—clean copy and reading aloud—but you must maintain a critical perspective. I'll give you now a list of things to check for, and I recommend that you *use* this list (going down it point by point, checking for each thing before you proceed to the next).

The Essay as a Whole

1. Does the thesis come out clearly? (See pages 2–4.)
2. Is the organization of the essay clear? (See pages 6–12.)
3. Is each paragraph unified? Is there anything in any of the paragraphs that doesn't belong? (See pages 6–12 and 15.)
4. Do the transitions work well within and between paragraphs?
5. Are arguments properly supported? Do I need to go back to the text for further evidence? (See pages 14–15 and 66–67.)
6. Does the introduction need to be rewritten to fit the body of the essay? (See pages 12–14.)
7. Is the conclusion effective? (See page 16.)

Sentence by Sentence

1. Check each sentence for deadwood, wordiness. Is each sentence clear? Is it concise? (See pages 16–20.)
2. Check for credibility. Do I believe this? Can I reasonably claim this? Watch out for hasty generalizations.
3. Run-ons and fragments. (See pages 86–87 and 89.) Have I written as a sentence something that is *more* than a sentence? *Less* than a sentence?
4. Agreement errors. (See pages 100–3 and 104–5.) Consciously identify the subject and verb of each sentence. Am I sure that the verb agrees with the *subject* of the sentence and not with some other noun that intervenes between subject and verb? Do my pronouns agree with their antecedents in gender and in number?
5. Parallelism and placement of modifiers. (See pages 106–10.) Have I messed up parallel constructions? Have I placed my modifiers as close as possible to the words they modify?
6. Punctuation. (See pages 89–97.) Check each sentence *very* carefully. Have I chosen the correct mark of punctuation? Have I set things off on both sides? Have I left out any necessary punctuation? Have I committed any intrusive comma errors? (See pages 90–91.)
7. Apostrophes. Have I used them properly? (See pages 95–97.)
8. Spelling. Have I checked for all possible spelling errors? Software spell-

checkers are good, but they cannot catch some of the more insidious spelling errors, nor do they catch problems like using "are" for "our," or accidentally dropping the "t" from "this" so that it reads "his." Proofread for these types of errors and always use a dictionary if you are uncertain of any spelling.

9. Handling and accuracy of quotations. (See pages 66–77.) Have I punctuated quotations correctly? Have I integrated them effectively into my own prose? Have I quoted accurately? (*Go back to the text to double-check.*)

10. Can I improve word choice? (See pages 20–21.)

11. How might I improve this essay by changing (and varying) sentence structure? (See pages 21–22.)

SAMPLE ESSAY

There is an analogy I like to use when I'm trying to explain how I arrive at a grade. Try thinking of your essay as a dive: you attempt a dive of a particular level of difficulty—it might be a simple dive or an extraordinarily difficult one—and then you *perform* it more or less well. To evaluate your performance fairly, I must take into consideration how challenging the task is that you have set yourself. On the one hand, an easy dive perfectly executed will obviously not be as impressive as a complex dive perfectly executed, or even as impressive as a complex dive performed with minor imperfections. On the other hand, a badly botched dive, no matter how tough it is, gets a lower score than an impeccably performed dive of moderate difficulty.

A paper that earns a grade of A can contain errors; an F paper can contain brilliant insights. There is no such thing really as a typical A, B, C, D, or F essay in an English course, since these grades are arrived at by weighing a number of factors:

1. grammar, punctuation, etc. (technical correctness)
2. quality of analysis
3. organization
4. use of evidence
5. style (effectiveness, precision, elegance)

A paper that gets top marks will be strong in all of these areas, though it will always (theoretically, at least) be possible to make the essay even better. But an essay that earns a C, for example, might be C-like in all five areas cited above, or A-like in one, F-like in another, and C-like in the remaining three. (I should acknowledge that in practice it is often impossible to untangle these factors from one another: strong analysis, for instance, cannot occur without appropriate evidence and will be unclear if the argument is poorly organized or if the sentences are so grammatically mangled that their meaning is unclear.)

What I'm going to do now is take a failing sample essay (probably worth no more than 40 percent) that is based on the story that follows and show you how it can be improved until after several versions it deserves an A grade.

Eudora Welty

Eudora Welty is a well-known American short-story writer and novelist. Born in 1909 in Jackson, Mississippi, to deeply Christian parents, she was immersed in the culture of the Southern states, and her work reflects this. It draws almost exclusively upon the landscape and social configurations of Mississippi. Welty is the author of the influential essay "Place in Fiction." Her most celebrated works include the novels *Delta Wedding* and *The Optimist's Daughter*, and a number of widely anthologized short stories such as "Why I Live at the P.O." and "A Worn Path."

EUDORA WELTY

A WORN PATH

It was December—a bright frozen day in the early morning. Far out in the country there was an old Negro woman with her head tied in a red rag, coming along a path through the pinewoods. Her name was Phoenix Jackson. She was very old and small and she walked slowly in the dark pine shadows, moving a little from side to side in her steps, with the balanced heaviness and lightness of a pendulum in a grandfather clock. She carried a thin, small cane made from an umbrella, and with this she kept tapping the frozen earth in front of her. This made a grave and persistent noise in the still air, that seemed meditative like the chirping of a solitary little bird.

She wore a dark striped dress reaching down to her shoe tops, and an equally long apron of bleached sugar sacks, with a full pocket: all neat and tidy, but every time she took a step she might have fallen over her shoelaces, which dragged from her unlaced shoes. She looked straight ahead. Her eyes were blue with age. Her skin had a pattern all its own of numberless branching wrinkles and as though a whole little tree stood in the middle of her forehead, but a golden color ran underneath, and the two knobs of her cheeks were illumined by

"A Worn Path" from *A Curtain of Green and Other Stories*, copyright 1941 and renewed 1969 by Eudora Welty. Reprinted by permission of Harcourt Brace & Company.

a yellow burning under the dark. Under the red rag her hair came down on her neck in the frailest of ringlets, still black, and with an odor like copper.

Now and then there was a quivering in the thicket. Old Phoenix said, "Out of my way, all you foxes, owls, beetles, jack rabbits, coons, and wild animals! . . . Keep out from under these feet, little bobwhites. . . . Keep the big wild hogs out of my path. Don't let none of those come running my direction. I got a long way." Under her small black-freckled hand her cane, limber as a buggy whip, would switch at the brush as if to rouse up any hiding things.

On she went. The woods were deep and still. The sun made the pine needles almost too bright to look at, up where the wind rocked. The cones dropped as light as feathers. Down in the hollow was the mourning dove—it was not too late for him.

The path ran up a hill. "Seem like there is chains about my feet, time I get this far," she said, in the voice of argument old people keep to use with themselves. "Something always take a hold of me on this hill—pleads I should stay."

After she got to the top she turned and gave a full, severe look behind her where she had come. "Up through the pines," she said at length. "Now down through oaks."

Her eyes opened their widest, and she started down gently. But before she got to the bottom of the hill a bush caught her dress.

Her fingers were busy and intent, but her skirts were full and long, so that before she could pull them free in one place they were caught in another. It was not possible to allow the dress to tear. "I in the thorny bush," she said. "Thorns, you doing your appointed work. Never want to let folks pass, no sir. Old eyes thought you was a pretty little *green* bush."

Finally, trembling all over, she stood free, and after a moment dared to stoop for her cane.

"Sun so high!" she cried, leaning back and looking, while the thick tears went over her eyes. "The time getting all gone here."

At the foot of this hill was a place where a log was laid across the creek.

"Now comes the trial," said Phoenix.

Putting her right foot out, she mounted the log and shut her eyes. Lifting her skirt, leveling her cane fiercely before her, like a festival figure in some parade, she began to march across. Then she opened her eyes and she was safe on the other side.

"I wasn't as old as I thought," she said.

But she sat down to rest. She spread her skirts on the bank around her and folded her hands over her knees. Up above her was a tree in a pearly cloud of mistletoe. She did not dare to close her eyes, and when a little boy brought her a plate with a slice of marble-cake on it she spoke to him. "That would be acceptable," she said. But when she went to take it there was just her own hand in the air.

So she left that tree, and had to go through a barbed-wire fence. There she had to creep and crawl, spreading her knees and stretching her fingers like a baby trying to climb the steps. But she talked loudly to herself: she could not let her dress be torn now, so late in the day, and she could not pay for having her arm or her leg sawed off if she got caught fast where she was.

At last she was safe through the fence and risen up out in the clearing. Big dead trees, like black men with one arm, were standing in the purple stalks of the withered cotton field. There sat a buzzard.

"Who you watching?"

In the furrow she made her way along.

"Glad this not the season for bulls," she said, looking sideways, "and the good Lord made his snakes to curl up and sleep in the winter. A pleasure I don't see no two-headed snake coming around that tree, where it come once. It took a while to get by him, back in the summer."

She passed through the old cotton and went into a field of dead corn. It whispered and shook and was taller than her head. "Through the maze now," she said, for there was no path.

Then there was something tall, black, and skinny there, moving before her.

At first she took it for a man. It could have been a man dancing in the field. But she stood still and listened, and it did not make a sound. It was as silent as a ghost.

"Ghost," she said sharply, "who be you the ghost of? For I have heard of nary death close by."

But there was no answer—only the ragged dancing in the wind.

She shut her eyes, reached out her hand, and touched a sleeve. She found a coat and inside that an emptiness, cold as ice.

"You scarecrow," she said. Her face lighted. "I ought to be shut up for good," she said with laughter. "My senses is gone. I too old. I the oldest people I ever know. Dance, old scarecrow," she said, "while I dancing with you."

She kicked her foot over the furrow, and with mouth drawn down, shook her head once or twice in a little strutting way. Some husks blew down and whirled in streamers about her skirts.

Then she went on, parting her way from side to side with the cane, through the whispering field. At last she came to the end, to a wagon track where the silver grass blew between the red ruts. The quail were walking around like pullets, seeming all dainty and unseen.

"Walk pretty," she said. "This the easy place. This the easy going."

She followed the track, swaying through the quiet bare fields, through the little strings of trees silver in their dead leaves, past cabins silver from weather, with the doors and windows boarded shut, all like old women under a spell sitting there. "I walking in their sleep," she said, nodding her head vigorously.

In a ravine she went where a spring was silently flowing through a hollow log. Old Phoenix bent and drank. "Sweet-gum makes the water sweet," she said, and drank more. "Nobody know who made this well, for it was here when I was born."

The track crossed a swampy part where the moss hung as white as lace from every limb. "Sleep on, alligators, and blow your bubbles." Then the track went into the road.

Deep, deep the road went down between the high green-colored banks. Overhead the live-oaks met, and it was as dark as a cave.

A black dog with a lolling tongue came up out of the weeds by the ditch. She was meditating and not ready, and when he came at her she only hit him a little with her cane. Over she went in the ditch, like a little puff of milkweed.

Down there, her senses drifted away. A dream visited her, and she reached her hand up, but nothing reached down and gave her a pull. So she lay there and presently went to talking. "Old woman," she said to herself, "that there black dog come up out of the weeds to stall you off, and now there he is sitting on his fine tail, smiling at you."

A white man finally came along and found her—a hunter, a young man, with his dog on a chain.

"Well, Granny!" he laughed. "What are you doing there?"

"Lying on my back like a June-bug waiting to be turned over, mister," she said, reaching up her hand.

He lifted her, gave her a swing in the air, and set her down. "Anything broken, Granny?"

"No sir, them old dead weeds is springy enough," said Phoenix, when she had got her breath. "I thank you for your trouble."

"Where do you live, Granny?" he asked, while the two dogs were growling at each other.

"Away back yonder, sir, behind the ridge. You can't even see it from here."

"On your way home?"

"No sir, I going to town."

"Why, that's too far! That's as far as I walk when I come out myself, and I get something for my trouble." He patted the stuffed bag he carried, and there hung down a little closed claw. It was one of the bobwhites, with its beak hooked bitterly to show it was dead. "Now you go on home, Granny!"

"I bound to go to town, mister," said Phoenix. "The time come around."

He gave another laugh, filling the whole landscape. "I know you old colored people! Wouldn't miss going to town to see Santa Claus!"

But something held old Phoenix very still. The deep lines in her face went into a fierce and different radiation. Without warning, she had seen with her own eyes a flashing nickel fall out of the man's pocket onto the ground.

"How old are you, Granny?" he was saying.

"There is no telling, mister," she said, "no telling."

Then she gave a little cry and clapped her hands and said, "Git on away from here, dog! Look! Look at that dog!" She laughed as if in admiration. "He ain't scared of nobody. He a big black dog." She whispered, "Sic him!"

"Watch me get rid of that old cur," said the man. "Sic him, Pete! Sic him!"

Phoenix heard the dogs fighting, and heard the man running and throwing sticks. She even heard a gunshot. But she was slowly bending forward by that time, further and further forward, the lid stretched down over her eyes, as if she were doing this in her sleep. Her chin was lowered almost to her knees. The yellow palm of her hand came out from the fold of her apron. Her fingers slid down and along the ground under the piece of money with the grace and care they would have in lifting an egg from under a setting hen. Then she slowly straightened up, she stood erect, and the nickel was in her apron pocket. A bird flew by. Her lips moved. "God watching me the whole time. I come to stealing."

The man came back, and his own dog panted about them. "Well, I scared him off that time," he said, and then he laughed and lifted his gun and pointed it at Phoenix.

She stood straight and faced him.

"Doesn't the gun scare you?" he said, still pointing it.

"No, sir, I seen plenty go off closer by, in my day, and for less than what I done," she said, holding utterly still.

He smiled, and shouldered the gun. "Well, Granny," he said, "you must be a hundred years old, and scared of nothing. I'd give you a dime if I had any money with me. But you take my advice and stay home, and nothing will happen to you."

"I bound to go on my way, mister," said Phoenix. She inclined her head in the red rag. Then they went in different directions, but she could hear the gun shooting again and again over the hill.

She walked on. The shadows hung from the oak trees to the road like curtains. Then she smelled wood-smoke, and smelled the river, and she saw a steeple and the cabins on their steep steps. Dozens of little black children whirled around her. There ahead was Natchez shining. Bells were ringing. She walked on.

In the paved city it was Christmas time. There were red and green electric lights strung and crisscrossed everywhere, and all turned on in the daytime. Old Phoenix would have been lost if she had not distrusted her eyesight and depended on her feet to know where to take her.

She paused quietly on the sidewalk where people were passing by. A lady came along in the crowd, carrying an armful of red-, green-, and silver-wrapped presents; she gave off perfume like the red roses in hot summer, and Phoenix stopped her.

"Please, missy, will you lace up my shoe?" She held up her foot.

"What do you want, Grandma?"

"See my shoe," said Phoenix. "Do all right for out in the country, but wouldn't look right to go in a big building."

"Stand still then, Grandma," said the lady. She put her packages down on the sidewalk beside her and laced and tied both shoes tightly.

"Can't lace 'em with a cane," said Phoenix. "Thank you, missy. I doesn't mind asking a nice lady to tie up my shoe, when I gets out on the street."

Moving slowly and from side to side, she went into the big building, and into a tower of steps, where she walked up and around and around until her feet knew to stop.

She entered a door, and there she saw nailed up on the wall the document that had been stamped with the gold seal and framed in the gold frame, which matched the dream that was hung up in her head.

"Here I be," she said. There was a fixed and ceremonial stiffness over her body.

"A charity case, I suppose," said an attendant who sat at the desk before her.

But Phoenix only looked above her head. There was sweat on her face, and the wrinkles in her skin shone like a bright net.

"Speak up, Grandma," the woman said. "What's your name? We must have your history, you know. Have you been here before? What seems to be the trouble with you?"

Old Phoenix only gave a twitch to her face as if a fly were bothering her.

"Are you deaf?" cried the attendant.

But then the nurse came in.

"Oh, that's just old Aunt Phoenix," she said. "She doesn't come for herself—she has a little grandson. She makes these trips just as regular as clockwork. She lives away back off the Old Natchez Trace." She bent down. "Well, Aunt Phoenix, why don't you just take a seat? We won't keep you standing after your long trip." She pointed.

The old woman sat down, bolt upright in the chair.

"Now, how is the boy?" asked the nurse.

Old Phoenix did not speak.

"I said, how is the boy?"

But Phoenix only waited and stared straight ahead, her face very solemn and withdrawn into rigidity.

"Is his throat any better?" asked the nurse. "Aunt Phoenix, don't you hear me? Is your grandson's throat any better since the last time you came for the medicine?"

With her hands on her knees, the old woman waited, silent, erect, and motionless, just as if she were in armor.

"You mustn't take up our time this way, Aunt Phoenix," the nurse said. "Tell us quickly about your grandson, and get it over. He isn't dead, is he?"

At last there came a flicker and then a flame of comprehension across her face, and she spoke.

"My grandson. It was my memory had left me. There I sat and forgot why I made my long trip."

"Forgot?" The nurse frowned. "After you came so far?"

Then Phoenix was like an old woman begging a dignified forgiveness for waking up frightened in the night. "I never did go to school, I was too old at the Surrender," she said in a soft voice. "I'm an old woman without an education. It was my memory fail me. My little grandson, he is just the same, and I forgot it in the coming."

"Throat never heals, does it?" said the nurse, speaking in a loud, sure voice to old Phoenix. By now she had a card with something written on it, a little list. "Yes. Swallowed lye. When was it?—January—two, three years ago—"

Phoenix spoke unasked now. "No, missy, he not dead, he just the same. Every little while his throat began to close up again, and he not able to swallow. He not get his breath. He not able to help himself. So the time come around, and I go on another trip for the soothing medicine."

"All right. The doctor said as long as you came to get it, you could have it," said the nurse. "But it's an obstinate case."

"My little grandson, he sit up there in the house all wrapped up, waiting by himself," Phoenix went on. "We is the only two left in the world. He suffer and it don't seem to put him back at all. He got a sweet look. He going to last. He wear a little patch quilt and peep out holding his mouth open like a little bird. I remembers so plain now. I not going to forget him again, no, the whole enduring time. I could tell him from all the others in creation."

"All right." The nurse was trying to hush her now. She brought her a bottle of medicine. "Charity," she said, making a check mark in a book.

Old Phoenix held the bottle close to her eyes, and then carefully put it into her pocket.

"I thank you," she said.

"It's Christmas time, Grandma," said the attendant. "Could I give you a few pennies out of my purse?"

"Five pennies is a nickel," said Phoenix stiffly.

"Here's a nickel," said the attendant.

Phoenix rose carefully and held out her hand. She received the nickel and then fished the other nickel out of her pocket and laid it beside the new one. She stared at her palm closely, with her head on one side.

Then she gave a tap with her cane on the floor.

"This is what come to me to do," she said. "I going to the store and buy my child a little windmill they sells, made out of paper. He going to find it hard to believe there such a thing in the world. I'll march myself back where he waiting, holding it straight up in this hand."

  She lifted her free hand, gave a little nod, turned around, and walked out of the doctor's office. Then her slow step began on the stairs, going down.

VERSION 1

Is she senile? Phoenix appears to inavertly wan-

der up and down her chosen path. A path she has

on numerous occassions worn down through the

years. Her destination is apparent, when she

leaves her country home. Phoenix is going to

collect the medication for her beloved grandson,

during her journey she encounter many obstacles

and finally ends up at the town, only to forget

why she came.

  Is she senile? The reader must wonder about

the old woman travelling such a great distance

alone. Dreaming of marble-cake and momentarily

thinking it is reality. ' . . . "That would be

acceptable", she said, 'but when she went to

take it there was just her own hand in the air."

(p.9) Is she senile? The people Phoenix meets

denote her as inferior, a grandma, granny, and

old woman. The white man with the gun says to

her, after inquiring her where-abouts and des-

tination, . . . "Now you go home granny.". . . "I

know you old coloured people wouldn't miss going

to town to see Santa Claus." (p.10) Phoenix

stops a nice white lady in town. She wants this

Handwritten annotations:
- split infinitive → (pointing to "inavertly")
- sp (under "inavertly")
- FRAG (left margin, pointing to "A path she has...years.")
- sp (under "occassions")
- /CS (right of "grandson,")
- verb (under "encounter")
- FRAG (right of "momentarily")
- Q (right margin, bracketing quotation)
- ∅ = delete punctuation
- sp = spelling
- FRAG = sentence fragment
- CS = comma splice
- verb = verb form incorrect
- Q = quotation inaccurate or mishandled
- about (above "inquiring")
- ∧ (caret after "inquiring")
- ∅ (over "man")
- sp (under "where-abouts")
- Q (right margin, bracketing second quotation)

woman to tie her shoelaces, for Phoenix is too old and cannot with a cane in hand. The woman asked . . . "What do you want grandma ?" (p.11) | Q

Phoenix speaks to herself and anything that moves on her path, even the imaginary creatures. 'Now and then there was a quivering in the thicket'. . . "Out of my way, all you foxes, owls, beetles, jack rabbits, coons and wild animals". . . (p.8) . . . "up through the pines", she said at length,", "Now down through the oaks." (p.8) Her <u>illussive</u> mind<s>s</s> causes the
       sp
reader to question her behavior. Is she senile? Phoenix has a mission, but <u>has forgot</u> what it was
                      Verb
once at the <u>doctors</u> office. She remembers the
          Poss
clinic, with the document<s>s</s> in the gold frame with the gold seal. Still Phoenix <u>has forgot</u> her
                                Verb
appointed calling. "My grandson. It was my memory that left me". . . (p.12) she answered, after | Q
much <u>persuassion</u> from the nurse and attendant at
      sp
the clinic.

Is she senile? No, I do not believe so. Phoenix makes excuses because she is old. <u>Yey</u>, she is
     sp   *sp*
<u>niether</u> senile <u>nor</u> a scared old woman. Phoenix
  pc
is cautious and anticipates that whatever she confronts on <s>O</s>the worn path<s>O</s> will not stall her journey. Phoenix has taken the path oft<u>en and</u>
                                       c.a.c.
she encounters<s>s</s> the same external conditions. Yet<s>,</s> her eyes <u>decieve</u> her ". . . old eyes thought
                    sp

• poss=
  possessive
  apostrophe

• pc=
  parallel
  construction

• c.a.c. =
  "comma and"
  construction
  between in-
  dependent
  clauses

you was a pretty little green bush. . . (p.8) you

scarecrow she said "my senses is gone. I too old"

(p.9) Phoenix depends on her feet, not her eyes

to direct herself. "Where she walked up and
         Pronoun

around and around, until her feet knew to stop."

(p 11)

    I believe that Phoenix's heart is what guides

her feet. She loves her grandson dearly and

believes that "We is the only two left in the

world". (p.12) The only two that counts in her
                      Pronoun *Verb*

life. Phoenix is not afraid to take the nickel

that fell from the white mans pocket. Nor is she
                            Poss

scared to ask for five pennies, which is another

nickle, from the attendant. Now the coins are
SP

worth a dime. Enough money to buy a paper wind-

mill from the store. "He going to find it hard to

believe there is such a thing in the world" (p12)

The journey this time was not for just medica-
                           PC

tion, from a doctor, but love, the ultimate

medicine. Is this senile?

Marginal annotations: Q; FRAG; FRAG; Q; • pronoun = wrong pronoun form

Comment

This essay is obviously very weak. In order to address the problems of argumentation and so on, I will provide a cleaned-up version. This Version 2 corrects the errors in grammar, punctuation, and spelling marked on Version 1. It also corrects the quotations, every one of which was faulty! Please remember that you *must* quote exactly. In proofreading your essay, *always* go back to the text to ensure that you've got every word and every mark of punctuation exactly as it was in the original. There is no excuse for making errors of this kind. Also learn how to handle quotation marks, page numbers, and punctuation with quotations. Errors remaining in Version 2 (and marked on this otherwise clean copy) are one redundant phrase and four words that were incorrectly chosen.

VERSION 2

#1 Is she senile? Phoenix appears to wander inadvertently up and down her chosen path, which she has worn down ⟨on numerous occasions⟩ through the years. Her destination is apparent when she leaves her country home. Phoenix is going to collect the medication for her beloved grandson. During her journey she encounters many obstacles and finally ends up at the town, only to forget why she came.

#2 Is she senile? The reader must wonder about the old woman travelling such a great distance alone, dreaming of marble-cake and momentarily thinking it is reality. "'That would be acceptable,' she said, but when she went to take it there was just her own hand in the air" (9). Is she senile? The people Phoenix meets <u>denote</u> her

ww
as inferior, a grandma, granny, and old woman. The white man with the gun says to her, after inquiring about her <u>whereabouts</u> and destination,

ww
"'Now you go on home, Granny! . . . I know you old coloured people! Wouldn't miss going to town to see Santa Claus!'" (10). Phoenix stops a nice

• ⟨ ⟩ = omit, redundant

• ww = wrong word

white lady in town. She wants this woman to tie her shoelaces, for Phoenix is too old and cannot with a cane in hand. The woman asks, "'What do you want, Grandma?'" (11).

#3 Phoenix speaks to herself and anything that moves on her path, even imaginary creatures. "Now and then there was a quivering in the thicket. Old Phoenix said, 'Out of my way, all you foxes, owls, beetles, jack rabbits, coons and wild animals!'" (8). "'Up through the pines,' she said at length. 'Now down through oaks'" (8). Her <u>illusive</u> mind causes the reader
_ww_
to question her behaviour. Is she senile? Phoenix has a mission but forgets what it is once at the doctor's office. She remembers the clinic with the document in the gold frame with the gold seal. Still Phoenix forgets her appointed calling. "'My grandson. It was my memory that left me'" (12), she answers, after much persuasion from the nurse and attendant at the clinic.

#4 Is she senile? No, I do not believe so. Phoenix makes excuses because she is old. Yet she is neither senile nor scared. Phoenix is cautious and <u>anticipates</u> that whatever she confronts on
_ww_
the worn path will not stall her journey. Phoenix has taken the path often, and she encounters the same external conditions. Yet her eyes deceive her: "'Old eyes thought you was a pretty

ww =
wrong
word

little <u>green</u> bush'" (8). "'You scarecrow,' she said. . . . 'My senses is gone. I too old'" (9). Phoenix depends on her feet, not her eyes, to direct her: "she walked up and around and around until her feet knew to stop" (11).

#5   I believe that Phoenix's heart is what guides her feet. She loves her grandson dearly and believes that "'We is the only two left in the world'" (12). They are the only two who count in her life. Phoenix is not afraid to take the nickel that fell from the white man's pocket. Nor is she scared to ask for five pennies, which is another nickel, from the attendant. Now the coins are worth a dime, which is enough money to buy a paper windmill from the store. "'He going to find it hard to believe there such a thing in the world'" (12). The journey this time was not just for medication from a doctor, but for love, the ultimate medicine. Is this senile?

Comment

I would say that Version 2 is worth around 60 percent. But I find this version hard to grade because it would be extremely unusual to find an essay so free of technical errors that is also so weak in argumentation. In the versions that follow, I will not introduce any further technical errors. You should not conclude, however, that the 20-percent spread between 40 percent in Version 1 and 60 percent in Version 2 represents the amount that technical errors can count in an assessment of your work. The correction of the errors in this case raises the mark by 20 percent, but if you were to *commit* errors as serious and plentiful as these in an essay that might otherwise have earned 85 percent, your essay would still fail. Technical errors can make the difference between an A and an F, but an essay that is totally free of technical errors could still be a failing essay.

Argumentation. The cleaned-up copy of Version 2 makes it easier for us to see what the writer of the essay might be trying to say and how the argument can be improved. Notice that I have used the word "argument"—but what *is* the argument of this essay? What is the writer trying to prove? The repeated question ("Is she senile?") and the answer given in paragraph 4 ("No, I do not believe so.") suggest that the writer's purpose is to convince the reader that Phoenix is not senile. One of the oddities of this essay is that although it lacks a clear thesis statement, the reader knows from the repeated rhetorical questions what the essay is about. The *topic* is senility, and the implicit *thesis* is that Phoenix is not senile.

Most English instructors insist that the introductory paragraph of the essay contain a thesis statement. I am relatively flexible on this point, since I find that in superb essays by professional literary critics it is often impossible to find a sentence at the start of the essay that sums up the author's thesis. Still, I advise students to formulate a thesis and state it clearly near the beginning. In almost all cases, to do so will strengthen your work. In this case, if the writer had attempted to develop a thesis statement, the inadequacy of the project might have become apparent, and the project might at that stage have been redefined. Remember that the goal of a critical essay is to convince the reader that the thesis is *worth* defending and that it has been defended well.

My criticism of Version 2 is not so much that the essay lacks a thesis as that the implicit thesis is not sufficiently interesting from a literary point of view, and not properly worked out. The writer's attempt at diagnosis on this matter seems a bit peculiar. Does the writer know enough about symptoms of senile dementia (the technically correct term) to assess whether Phoenix is senile? Isn't senility a degenerative disorder, which gets worse over time (so that a person could be a bit senile but not totally so)? Does a defence of Phoenix require us to establish the truth or falsehood of this diagnosis? How important is this question? Is that really what the writer *wants* to work out? If so, we might expect a definition of senility and a list of symptoms to be found (or not found) in Phoenix.

Here is what I think might have gone on in the mind of the student who submitted Version 1. (I'll assume that the student was female.) In reading the story, she noticed that this very old woman was doing some peculiar things—talking to shrubs, hallucinating about marble-cake, and so on. Not surprisingly, she wondered whether Phoenix might be senile. To begin with, remember, she would have had no idea where Phoenix was going or whether this journey along the worn path made any sense. By the end of the story, her respect for Phoenix had naturally increased. She wanted in some way to account for her own earlier suspicions, while at the same time expressing admiration for Phoenix Jackson. But she didn't think the problem through before she began. She relied on the repeated question ("Is she senile?") to establish an easy structure for the essay. The technical carelessness of Version 1 is a symptom of the student's hurried approach to the task at hand; it is matched by her lack of care with the argument.

Now let's look at the function of each of the paragraphs in Version 2.

Please reread each paragraph of Version 2 before reading my analysis of it!

Paragraph 1

The student states incorrectly that "Her destination is apparent when she leaves her country home." In fact, Phoenix's destination and purpose are not revealed to the reader until the end of the story. But in the previous sentence the student seems to be recounting the experience of a reader who doesn't know the ending yet, when she says that "Phoenix appears to wander inadvertently up and down her chosen path . . ." I find myself confused. Is Phoenix just wandering "inadvertently" (without choice or conscious purpose), or is she consciously pursuing a "chosen path"? The two points contradict each other. I think the confusion arises because the student is not distinguishing between what she thought at the beginning and what she learned later. Or she may be reproducing a confusion she felt all along, since Phoenix might well have seemed determined *and* befuddled. (Notice also that the phrase "on numerous occasions" is redundant. It should be omitted, since "worn down" and "through the years" make the point by themselves.)

This paragraph asks the question ("Is she senile?") and does not answer it. On dramatic grounds, I could defend the student's decision not to answer the question (or state her thesis) in the first paragraph. She sets up the problem by offering one sample piece of evidence opposing the senility idea (Phoenix has a rational purpose: "medication for her beloved grandson") and another piece supporting it ("only to forget why she came"). These bits of evidence are well chosen because they serve another purpose too: they orient us to the story, giving a kind of miniature plot summary in an economical way. The main thing that is wrong with this paragraph is the confusion I describe above.

Paragraph 2 (Reread it first.)

Probably the intention of this paragraph (and the next) is to set out evidence that might lead the reader to think Phoenix is senile. But how well does the student *analyze* this evidence? Can I be sure that she intends it as evidence that Phoenix might be senile? Mainly, it feels like plot summary. If it were not for the repeated question ("Is she senile?"), the reader would have no idea that it formed any part of an argument. The first attempt at evidence is not too bad: the reader "must wonder" about the old woman travelling so far alone and about the cake dream. But the references to the hunter and the lady do not in any clear way show that Phoenix might be senile, and the student does not tell us why she thinks they do. She fails to analyze the evidence.

These two references are introduced by the statement that the people Phoenix meets "denote her as inferior"—presumably *because* she is old, since the student goes on to say "a grandma, granny, and old woman." Can you see that "denote" is the wrong word here? The people do not "denote" or (a better word) *call* her "inferior," though they do use the other three terms—"Granny," "Grandma," and "old colored people" (rather than "old woman"—so that's another error!). Try *regard* or *see* to cover all four cases: "The people Phoenix meets *see* her as inferior, *calling* her grandma, granny, and old woman." But note that the student has put these terms in the wrong order; they *should* occur in the order of their appearance in the quotations that follow. In Version 3 I change this to "a granny, an old coloured person, a grandma." (Incidentally, the word "whereabouts" is marked as wrong because what the hunter actually asks is where she *lives;* her "whereabouts" is her present location, which is a ditch!)

But what does any of that have to do with evidence of *senility?* Has the student switched topics here? If so, has she switched from senility to *old age* (failing to make a distinction between the two) or has she switched from senility to *inferiority?* Could it be that she's less interested in whether Phoenix is senile than in the larger question of what might lead us into the error of thinking that Phoenix is a person unworthy of our respect? (This worries me. Does she think old people or people suffering from senility are generally unworthy of respect? Couldn't Phoenix be afflicted by senility *and* be a heroine?)

I can't tell whether the student has detected and is trying to demonstrate through the quoted dialogue the racial condescension of the hunter and the lady. If she doesn't recognize the racial condescension, can we trust her understanding of the quoted material? The student is right in indicating that the hunter and the lady regard Phoenix as an inferior. But is that just because she's old or because she's black? Since the student hasn't given any interpretation of the dialogue she quotes, I don't know whether she has considered the latter possibility. (The dialogue suggests to me that they condescend for both reasons. Terms like "Granny" were used in the South only for blacks, unless the person in question really was your grandmother.) If race is part of what she is getting at here, how does it connect with the topic of old age and senility? In the beginning of this paragraph the idea of inferiority was tied to old age, but the issue of race complicates this. (You must always be certain that the *point* of a quotation is clear.)

Paragraph 3 (Reread it first.)

In this paragraph, the student points out (in a good topic sentence) that "Phoenix speaks to herself and anything that moves on her path, even imaginary creatures." She then supplies some good textual evidence, and offers a comment on it: "Her illusive mind causes the reader to question her behaviour. Is she senile?" (The word "illusive" is a rarely used adjective; "illusory" has the same meaning and is much more common. It means that the thing it modifies—in this case, Phoenix's mind—is an illusion. This is obviously not what the student intends. She might say instead that "Phoenix's illusions cause the reader to question her behaviour." But is it really her *behaviour* that comes into question? What the student means, I think, is simply this: "Phoenix's illusions cause the reader to think she may be senile.")

I wonder why the marble-cake hallucination doesn't come here (rather than in the second paragraph). Another problem with paragraph unity is that the student now leaves the subject of illusion and returns to the fact that when Phoenix gets to the doctor's office she forgets her mission. Also, the detail here feels too much like plot summary.

Paragraph 4 (Reread it first.)

Now nearing the end of the essay, the student tells us that she doesn't believe Phoenix is senile. She doesn't dispose of the evidence to the contrary that she has assembled in the previous paragraphs, except by saying that Phoenix must make excuses because she is old. (And I wonder if that's true. Does Phoenix really try to make excuses for herself? I would say rather that she acknowledges the infirmity that comes with age. The student does not tell us what excuses she makes.) As evidence against senility, she offers this comment: "Phoenix is cautious and anticipates that whatever she confronts on the worn path will not stall her journey." (Notice that the word "anticipates" is wrong. Do you see how this sentence snaps into focus if you substitute the adjective "determined"?)

In the second half of the paragraph, the student seems to return to the infirmity of old age, as she points out that Phoenix's "eyes deceive her"— even though "she encounters the same external conditions" whenever she walks on this path. (But that isn't true; the dangers and pleasures vary with the seasons, as Phoenix herself points out.) The scarecrow is mentioned without apparent purpose, although the quotation goes on to supply further evidence that Phoenix acknowledges the infirmity of age. The final quotation ("her feet knew to stop") shows that she can rely on her feet even if her eyes fail.

Paragraph 5 (Reread it first.)

The concluding paragraph begins with an excellent transition from paragraph 4: "I believe that Phoenix's heart is what guides her feet." The general topic of this paragraph is love. The student establishes the intense focus of Phoenix's love with the quotation "'We is the only two left in the world,'" and goes on to say that Phoenix is "not afraid" to steal and beg the money to buy the paper windmill. The student does not state that love gives Phoenix this courage, though I'm sure that's what she means. She might also point out that love makes Phoenix determined and resourceful.

The lovely quotation describing the grandson's predicted wonder over the gift helps to provide a feeling of intensity for the conclusion of the essay. (But what it actually *says* hasn't been analyzed or used.) The next sentence—about love as "the ultimate medicine"—is also dramatically effective. But what does she mean by this exactly? Does love (as the ultimate medicine) cure the grandson or Phoenix? Remember that love is being offered as the final argument against senility, so it would seem that it "cures" Phoenix. But the student doesn't indicate this because she hasn't thought through her own analogy (love = medicine). And why is the journey undertaken "this time" for love, rather than for ordinary medicine? Haven't all of Phoenix's previous journeys demonstrated her love? The difference this time is that she also brings back the windmill. Certainly that is a gift of love, but so is the medicine. (Actually, I'm not sure whether the student *means* me to connect the windmill and "this time . . . for love.")

The final sentence varies the refrain slightly: "Is this senile?" The answer is supposed to be self-evident. The student thinks that Phoenix's love and the gift of the windmill prove that she isn't senile, so she rests her case there.

Now I will improve the quality of analysis, the organization, and the use of evidence for Version 3. First, though, let's think about a refinement of the implicit thesis from Version 2 (*Phoenix is not senile*). I suggest the following: *Especially before they get to the end of the story, readers may wonder if Phoenix is senile. But in the end it seems that Phoenix's love and determination are so strong that even if she is a little senile, old age cannot defeat her.* It's helpful to write down a statement like this, even if you don't end up using it in exactly that form once you get down to the job of writing.

In the version that follows I use little more than was provided in the original essay. The improvements come from testing and then revising or omitting certain statements in the original essay, from looking harder at the quotations used, and *most of all* from refining the argument and presenting it in a logical order.

Here now is a brief outline for Version 3:

Paragraph 1. Introduction
    – set up situation
    – effect on reader of not knowing P's goal until end
    – thesis

Paragraph 2. Evidence of possible senility (illusions)

    – talking to herself
    – marble-cake
    – scarecrow (but turn toward P's awareness of problem)

Paragraph 3. More evidence? (other characters)

    – hunter ("Granny" & "old colored people")
    – lady ("Grandma")
    – *but* note racism too & P's success in dealing w/it (fit in nickel from hunter somewhere); thus she comes out on top.

Paragraph 4. Conclusion (love triumphs over age)

    – "too old"
    – eyes fail her, but feet take over
    – heart guides feet
    – gets what she came for even though she forgets
    – also money for windmill
    – her love is what seems really "hard to believe"
    – love is ultimate medicine, for him & her

VERSION 3

Is Phoenix senile? As she travels along her chosen path, Phoenix knows what her destination is. She is going to collect medicine for her beloved grandson. But we don't know this. To us, her journey may seem foolish and without purpose. Phoenix often seems out of touch with reality, and the other characters she meets see her as incompetent. Finally, she gets to town, only to forget why she came. But by this time, it is clear to the reader that Phoenix's love and determination are so strong that even if she is a little senile, old age cannot defeat her.

Phoenix speaks to herself and anything that moves on her path, even imaginary creatures. "Now and then there was a quivering in the thicket. Old Phoenix said, 'Out of my way, all you foxes, owls, beetles, jack rabbits, coons and wild animals!'" (8). At one point, she has a hallucination about a little boy serving her a slice of marble-cake: "'That would be acceptable,' she said, but when she went to take it there was just her own hand in the air" (9). At another point, she talks to a scarecrow she has mistaken for a ghost. All of this might be taken as evidence of senility. However, in her speech to the scarecrow, it is clear that Phoenix is aware of the problem: "'I ought to be shut up for good,' she said with laughter. 'My senses is gone. I too old'" (9).

The people Phoenix meets regard her as an inferior, a granny, an old coloured person, a grandma. The white man with the gun, who lifts her up when she falls on the path, seems to think Phoenix is too old to be out alone, and that she has entered her second childhood: "'Now you go on home, Granny! . . . I know you old colored people! Wouldn't miss going to town to see Santa Claus!'" (10). When she gets to town, Phoenix cannot tie her own shoes because of the cane in her hand. The white lady who ties them for her also speaks to Phoenix in a condescending way, asking, "'What do you want, Grandma?'" (11) even though "Grandma" has already told her. These characters look down on Phoenix because of her age and her race, but readers may not want to follow their example. What we notice most is that she is determined to get what she needs (including the nickel that the hunter drops) and is not ashamed to ask for help. In fact, Phoenix seems to come out on top in these scenes.

Is Phoenix senile? Perhaps she is a bit, but that doesn't stop her. Since Phoenix is "'the oldest people I ever know'" (9), her eyes may deceive her: "'Old eyes thought you was a pretty little green bush'" (8). But Phoenix depends on her feet, not her eyes, to achieve her goal: "she walked up and around and around until her feet knew to stop" (11). I believe that Phoenix's heart is what guides her feet. At the end of the story, just as Phoenix achieves her goal, she forgets why she came. But she does finally remember: "'My grandson. It was my memory that left me'" (12). She gets the medicine, and she also cleverly gets another five pennies from the attendant, so that now she has enough money to buy a paper windmill as a Christmas present for her grandson: "'He going to find it hard to believe there such a thing in the world'" (12). At this point, the reader may find it hard to believe that there can be love as strong as Phoenix's in this world. Love, the ultimate medicine, triumphs over the sickness of old age and--along with the medicine and the windmill--goes home with Phoenix to her grandson.

Comment

This essay is probably worth an A. It is entirely free of technical errors, it has a reasonable thesis, and it is clear and beautifully organized. However, it doesn't contain any surprises, except for the last sentence, which is very sophisticated. Try to imagine Version 3 with a few technical errors and without that great last sentence, and you'll have an essay in the B range.

In the next and final version, I show you what happens when the student comes up with truly exciting ideas about the text. Version 4 would certainly be a high A+. In fact, it would be extremely unusual to find an essay as sophisticated and as polished as this one in an introductory English course. (It would be good work coming from a graduate student, so please don't be alarmed!) However, it is *not* unusual for a first-year essay to contain some great ideas. Real insights about the text can have a considerable impact upon your grade; it may be possible for an essay that contains such ideas to falter a bit on the organizational and technical side and *still* get an A.

Readers of "A Worn Path" may question whether Phoenix Jackson is a senile and incompetent wanderer or a heroic old woman who is in charge of her life's journey. Only at the end of the story do we learn that she travels her long and difficult path in pursuit of medicine for her beloved grandson. It is interesting that the strongest evidence of senility also comes at this point, when her heroism is most clearly revealed. Phoenix forgets for a moment the thing that is most important to her: her grandson and the purpose of her long walk. This juxtaposition may cause the reader to reflect upon the connection between such setbacks and the triumph of Phoenix. I would argue that the difficulties this extraordinary individual has experienced through her long life as an impoverished black woman in the South, to which are now added the humiliations of old age, have actually served to strengthen her spirit.

Phoenix talks to herself and to animals who may or may not be there: "Now and then there was a quivering in the thicket. Old Phoenix said, 'Out of my way, all you foxes, owls, beetles, jack rabbits, coons and wild animals!'" (8). Tired out, she has a vision of marble-cake being served to her by a little boy, "but when she went to take it there was just her own hand in the air" (9). She also mistakes a scarecrow for a ghost. We might be tempted to condescend to Phoenix and to see such occasions as indicating a loss of contact with reality or as evidence of senility, but these examples could also suggest that old Phoenix is extraordinarily sensitive to the natural and supernatural worlds. The other characters in the story seem to look down on Phoenix and are ready to dismiss her, partly because she is so old. The hunter tries to send her home, exclaiming, "'I know you old colored people! Wouldn't miss going to town to see Santa Claus!'" (10). The irony is that he is dead wrong, because Phoenix has a serious reason for going to town. The hunter is clearly guilty of racism and ageism in applying this infantile stereotype to Phoenix. Ironically too, Phoenix manages to get a coin he claimed he didn't have, and she will use it to buy a Christmas present for someone who really is a child.

"'What do you want, Grandma?'" asks the lady who eventually bends to tie Phoenix's shoes, making her repeat a clear request, and treating her like an incompetent child: "'Stand still then, Grandma'" (11). In this second example too, sterotypes of race and age strive to make the real Phoenix invisible, but the careful and sympathetic reader should not succumb. Ironically, black Phoenix takes advantage of her age to manipulate the white woman into kneeling before her.

Phoenix has presumably had trouble all her life because she is black, and now she is looked down upon also because she is old. But she triumphs in spite of that. Interestingly, despite their condescension and her failing senses, Phoenix can see and hear and speak her desires much more clearly than the young white people in the story. This recognition may cause us to think again about Phoenix's supposed senile hallucinations. Perhaps at this late stage in her life, Phoenix is able not only to operate successfully in the reality she is confronted with (a racist society), but also to glimpse the supernatural reality that awaits her. In heaven, Phoenix will rest and be served her reward of marble-cake by angels or by the child she has loved so tenderly in this world.

The scarecrow she has danced with all her life is the racism that attempts to scare off needy and insistent black creatures like Phoenix (and the crow); the scarecrow she (an old crow) is dancing with in her old age is death. Phoenix knows that her senses are failing--knows that soon she will be "'shut down for good'" and that she is "'too old'" (9)--but she laughs in the face of death, dances, and perseveres. If her eyes fail, she can depend on her feet: "she walked up and around and around until her feet knew to stop" (11). If her memory fails, she can depend on the extraordinary power of her determined heart, which takes Phoenix infallibly along the worn path to the doctor's office and earns her the reward she seeks above all.

This simple medication can soothe the throat of a child who has swallowed lye, as people like Phoenix and her grandson have been made to swallow all kinds of hardship, because it represents love, life's ultimate medicine. Hardships, we may conclude, such as racial prejudice and the infirmity of old age, may be overcome through the power of love--which is tested and strengthened by adversity.

Comment

This essay is remarkable because it has attempted a very hard dive and accomplished it almost perfectly. The style is now more elegant, more polished; the structure is more complex because more ideas are being developed. Notice some of the new things that are here.

Paragraph 1

A sophisticated *literary* point is made in the first paragraph, concerning the "juxtaposition" of the strongest evidence of senility and the revelation of Phoenix's heroism. Seeing that these things are next to each other in the text, the writer asks *why*—and comes up with a good answer. The thesis (last sentence) goes beyond arguing that old age cannot defeat Phoenix. It now argues something much more difficult: that hardships such as old age and racism have actually *strengthened* her spirit.

Paragraph 2

This paragraph (now in a new position within the essay) makes the interesting suggestion that Phoenix's illusions may hint at a spiritual strength.

Paragraph 3

The irony of the hunter's remark about Santa Claus has been pointed out. We are also led to see the much more subtle irony of the fact that the hunter's nickel will buy some "Santa Claus" for a real child. (Attention to irony is often a mark of *literary* sophistication.)

Paragraph 4

The issue of racism is skilfully interwoven with ageism in this paragraph about the lady (now split off from the hunter because the essay has more to say about each). Another subtle irony is pointed out: that a white woman is manipulated into kneeling before a black woman. You might object that she doesn't necessarily *kneel*, or that this is probably not Phoenix's aim. But the point is still quite a nifty one, and it may very well be that the author wanted us to appreciate this tableau.

Paragraph 5

The idea that Phoenix comes out on top has now been extended to make the interesting suggestion that her failing senses are nonetheless stronger than those of the hunter and the lady. This point is valid, but it would be nice to have some examples. (They have been left out because the essay was getting too long; the writer is struggling hard to be concise because she has a great deal to say.) Notice how the essay tracks the effect of certain observations on the *reader*—if we notice that Phoenix's senses are actually quite strong, we may then "think again" about her senile hallucinations. The essay returns to the marble-cake (discussed in an earlier paragraph) now that the groundwork has been laid for a more interesting suggestion (that the little boy might be the grandson in heaven). The connection of race and age becomes even more sophisticated as the essay associates racism with this world and suggests that old age will deliver Phoenix into a better world hereafter.

Paragraph 6

The essay also returns to the scarecrow now that more groundwork has been laid. Having paused to think a little about scarecrows, the writer has taken note of the fact that crows are black and hungry, and that people who own land set up straw men to scare them off. She can therefore make a fascinating and persuasive connection between crows and black people, and between scarecrows and racism. (She might also have recalled the "Jim Crow" laws, which protected segregation.) She has remembered that old people are sometimes called old crows, and she is apparently aware of the traditional literary images of death as a scarecrow and of dancing with death. Thus, she is able to use this scarecrow to confirm her sense that the issues of racism and old age are deeply intertwined in this story.

Paragraph 7

The conclusion of the essay builds on the idea of love as the ultimate medicine and takes account of its effect on Phoenix, as Version 3 failed to do. Particularly striking is the fact that the writer has stopped to think about the lye swallowed by the grandson, and has *used* that (lye = hardship; think of a throat and the terrible things each has had to "swallow") to show that love (the ultimate medicine) eases the tortured path of life for both Phoenix and her grandson. The analogy is concisely expressed, and it works well.

The final sentence reminds us of the claim made in the thesis statement: that Phoenix's spirit has been strengthened by adversity. This conclusion has been prepared for by the writer's insistence on how well Phoenix manages in the circumstances of her age and race. But now in a *very* concise statement (the last sentence of Version 4) she shows how the idea works. Ideally, the writer takes more time to make this point. I will elaborate, so that you can take in the logic of what she is saying in this last sentence.

(1) Hardships can be "overcome through the power of love." That is, love can keep her going in very difficult circumstances. Thus, Phoenix's love for her grandson is such that in her eyes "'We is the only two left in the world'" (12); because she focuses on the intensity of her love for him, she can brush off insults and threats from bigots like the hunter. Thus, too, she can travel a path that ought to be impossible for an extremely old woman *because* she loves her grandson too much to let him down. The hardships of

"racial prejudice and the infirmity of old age" are in this way "overcome through the power of love."

(2) Love is "tested and strengthened by adversity." Obviously *she* is tested by adversity, but so is her love. Love keeps her going, and a failure in love would stop her. The weights that her love must push hard against in this lifelong test are "adversity"; because her love is exercised so thoroughly, because it contends with such heavy weights, it is "strengthened" (as any muscle is strengthened by exercise).

(3) Phoenix's "spirit" (to return to the term used in the thesis statement) is "strengthened by adversity" because love is strengthened by it (as shown above) *and* because other qualities—courage, determination, cleverness— are also called into play and strengthened by the powerful insistence of her love. Together, these qualities make up her spirit. She needs these things if she is "'going to last'" (12)—as her grandson, with his "'sweet look'" of love, is also going to last.

FINAL COMMENTS

Original ideas. I have assumed in assigning grades to the four versions of the sample essay that the ideas contained in them have not simply been recycled from lectures and tutorials. This does not mean that you cannot use such ideas; it *does* mean that your essay should go beyond them. Consider the new ideas that are introduced in Version 4. If the ideas about the scarecrow, for example, had been given in the lecture, there would be no merit in simply repeating them in an essay. If nothing had been said about the scarecrow, the essay would be particularly impressive; if something had been pointed out— perhaps that the scarecrow is an image of death or that crows (like Phoenix) are black—the essay would still be impressive because it extends these ideas and situates them within an argument.

Titles. I have not so far given a title to any of these essays. However, you should always provide a title. Your instructor may wish you to indicate in some way which topic you are addressing, if you are choosing from an assigned list. But only rarely will the exact wording of the topic provide you with a good title. For example, "The Extent to Which Old Age and Racism Are Related Issues in 'A Worn Path'" is a poor title for Version 4; "Old Age and Racism in 'A Worn Path'" is better, and perfectly satisfactory—but you may find it a little dull. The title should give the reader some idea of what the essay is about. If I wanted a more imaginative title for Version 4—let's say, "Phoenix and the Scarecrow"—I could *combine* that with a more obvious signal of the essay's content by using a colon.

Phoenix and the Scarecrow:
Old Age and Racism in "A Worn Path"

"Phoenix and the Scarecrow" would have been a fine title all by itself if the essay had been primarily focused on the scarecrow. In the case of Version 4, "Phoenix and the Scarecrow" could not be used alone; as *half* the title, however, it serves the useful purpose of directing the reader's attention to how the scarecrow encapsulates (for this essay) the two themes of old age and racism.

Works cited. I have so far left out the Works Cited section of the essay, which comes at the end. In a short essay, you may choose to put this on the last page—if there is enough room. This saves trees. For all versions of the sample essay, you would type a dividing line (row of equal-signs or hyphens) and write as follows:

Works Cited

Welty, Eudora. "A Worn Path." *Reading Our World: The Guelph Anthology.* Eds. Constance Rooke, Renée Hulan, and Linda Warley. Needham Heights: Ginn, 1990. 8-12.

POETRY
EXPLICATION

You may be asked at some point to write a poetry explication. To explicate means to make clear or to explain. What you need to do if you are writing this kind of essay, then, is to explain or analyze, concisely and in detail, the main features of the poem you are working on. As with any formal English essay, you should have in your introduction a thesis that provides the focus of the essay. The paragraphs following the introduction should support the argument that you present in your thesis.

Not all poems look difficult at first glance, but many do. And some keep on looking difficult. The language of poetry is often dense and strange, and the meaning may seem cryptic. You may find yourself irritated by what seems to be willful obscurity. In the case of a really good poem, however, any apparent obscurity is actually a function of the poet's need to bend our minds a little—so that fresh perceptions will be possible. Don't panic! And don't expect an immediate, full revelation of the meaning of the poem. Understanding takes time, and the meaning will come to you in stages. (The poet T.S. Eliot observed that "poetry communicates before it is understood"— and I think that's true.)

As you read the poem over and over, different things will occur to you: you start making connections and noticing patterns, and eventually the layers of meaning begin to reveal themselves. After you have read the poem over to yourself a few times, be sure to read it aloud—you'll be amazed by what you suddenly understand when you can *hear* the poem.

There are a few standard questions you might want to ask yourself when you are working on an explication. These are things you need to know in order to understand generally what is going on in the poem. Ask yourself: Who is speaking? What is the tone of the poem? (Tone is the implied attitude of the author.) What is interesting about the language of the poem? Do the images form patterns? How do those patterns contribute to the meaning of the poem? Are the images a kind of language through which an idea is being explored by the poet? Is one idea struggling against another in this poem? How does the structure of the poem—the organization into stanzas, and within stanzas—help to create meaning? How do technical features like rhyme, alliteration, or assonance contribute to the feeling and meaning of the poem?

Obviously you cannot include *everything* you notice about the poem in your explication. What you need to do is strike a balance between reasonable coverage and the focused development of a thesis—the particular path you are taking through the poem. It's important in an explication to deal with specific details. Be sure to avoid generalities that get you too far away from the text. (Your instructor will suspect that you are doing this because you can't cope with the details!)

While you need to get some distance on the poem—so that you can see the forest as well as the trees—you *must* pay close attention to the individual components that make up the poem as a whole. One of the great things about analyzing a short poem (as opposed to a novel, say) is that all the words are there in front of you at once; it's possible to survey the whole thing. You can keep on going over and over those details until you see how the whole poem works.

Read "Cook's Mountains" through a few times. Then look at how I have marked up the poem, paying special attention to structure and sound and the dominant image pattern. It's a good idea to make several photocopies of a poem you're working on, so that you can mark it up several times. This is the all-important brainstorming phase. Keep pushing yourself. If you quit too soon, your essay will be weak. Keep pushing yourself. Don't forget to get rid of the ideas that on further reflection seem not to work. And don't feel that you have to use everything that occurs to you—but do get a lot of ideas down, so that you can be choosey!

P.K. Page

P.K. Page (1916–) is a distinguished Canadian poet, prose writer, and painter. In 1954 she won the Governor General's Award for Poetry for *The Metal and the Flower*. Other volumes of poetry include *Cry Ararat, Evening Dance of the Grey Flies, The Glass Air,* and *Hologram*. "Cook's Mountains" comes out of a period in which Page was living in Australia, where her husband was Canada's High Commissioner.

COOK'S MOUNTAINS

By naming them he made them.
They were there
before he came
but they were not the same.
It was his gaze
that glazed each one.
He saw
the Glass House Mountains in his glass.
They shone.

And still they shine.
We saw them as we drove—
sudden, surrealist, conical
they rose
out of the rain forest.
The driver said,
"Those are the Glass House Mountains up ahead."

And instantly they altered to become
the sum of shape and name.
Two strangenesses united into one
more strange than either.
Neither of us now
remembers how they looked before they broke
the light into fragments as the driver spoke.

Like mounds of mica,
hive-shaped hothouses,
mountains of mirror glimmering
they form
in diamond panes behind the tree ferns of
the dark imagination,
burn and shake
the lovely light of Queensland like a bell
reflecting Cook upon a deck
his tongue
silvered with paradox and metaphor.

P.K. Page

"Cook's Mountains" is reprinted by permission of the author.

Now let's see what we can do with it . . .

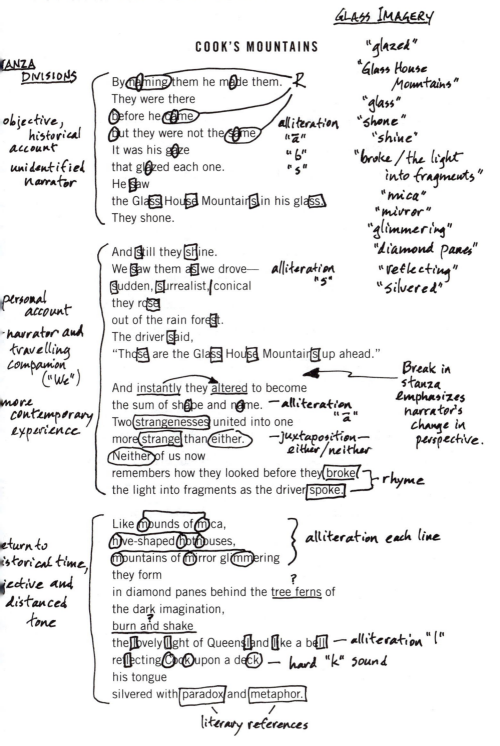

GLASS IMAGERY

"glazed"
"Glass House Mountains"
"glass"
"shone"
"shine"
"broke / the light into fragments"
"mica"
"mirror"
"glimmering"
"diamond panes"
"reflecting"
"silvered"

COOK'S MOUNTAINS

STANZA DIVISIONS

objective, historical account
unidentified narrator

By naming them he made them.
They were there
before he came,
but they were not the same.
It was his gaze
that glazed each one.
He saw
the Glass House Mountains in his glass.
They shone.

R

alliteration
"ā"
"b"
"s"

personal account
- narrator and travelling companion ("We")

more contemporary experience

And still they shine.
We saw them as we drove—
sudden, surrealist, conical
they rose
out of the rain forest.
The driver said,
"Those are the Glass House Mountains up ahead."

alliteration
"s"

And instantly they altered to become
the sum of shape and name.
Two strangenesses united into one
more strange than either.
Neither of us now
remembers how they looked before they broke
the light into fragments as the driver spoke.

— alliteration "ā"
— juxtaposition — either/neither

Break in stanza emphasizes narrator's change in perspective.

rhyme

return to historical time, objective and distanced tone

Like mounds of mica,
hive-shaped hothouses,
mountains of mirror glimmering
they form   ?
in diamond panes behind the tree ferns of
the dark imagination,
burn and shake   ?
the lovely light of Queensland like a bell — alliteration "l"
reflecting Cook upon a deck — hard "k" sound
his tongue
silvered with paradox and metaphor.

} alliteration each line

literary references

POETRY EXPLICATION   59

THE PARADOX OF LANGUAGE:
AN EXPLICATION OF P.K. PAGE'S
"COOK'S MOUNTAINS"

As the title of the poem suggests, "Cook's Mountains" is a poem about possession. It is also about the transition from a pre-verbal state to a "named" or verbal state. The poem points to the paradox of naming: while naming is creative and powerful, it is also limiting. Once named, an object snaps into focus. But the name interferes as well: it comes <u>between</u> us and the object. We can think of the object now only through the name that has been attached to it. The opening line of the poem, "By naming them he made them," connects "naming" with making. The poem suggests that things are unformed until they are "named." This idea--that naming <u>makes</u> an object--is paradoxical since the "making" is both creative and destructive. Naming reduces the range of possible meanings that exist when the object is understood only through the senses. By naming the mountains Cook has changed them; this alteration is emphasized by the rhyming of "name," "came," and "not the same."

The use of glass imagery begins with the rhyme of "gaze" and "glaze." When "he saw" the mountains, Cook "glazed" them; that is, he turned them to glass. The shortness of the line "He saw" emphasizes the importance of both Cook and the act of seeing; he did all this by seeing. The line "the Glass House Mountains in his glass" associates Cook's way of seeing--looking through a spyglass--with what he sees. In other words, the mountains may look like glass to Cook because he is looking at them through glass. From now on, this is what the name "Glass House Mountains" will do. It determines what we can see. The appropriateness of the name seems to be proclaimed by the final short line in the stanza: "They shone."

In the second stanza, the poem switches tone and point of view and describes the narrator's memory of seeing the mountains that still "shine." She describes them as she first sees them: "sudden, surrealist, and conical." They rise "out of the rain forest," out of a place of fertility and life. But then the driver announces that "[t]hose are the Glass House Mountains up ahead." A break occurs in the narrator's mind when she hears the name. This break is signalled by the stanza break and acknowledged in the next line: "And instantly they altered to become / the sum of shape and name." The mountains have been remade for her by the driver's statement. They become "two strangenesses": one is the shape of the mountains themselves and the other is the "name" that Cook gave them. Hearing the name of the mountain changes the narrator's relationship to them. She no longer has an image of them that is purely visual and sensual; the name has given her a specific way of looking at the mountains.

The mountains have become associated with glass and reflection: "mounds of mica," "hive-shaped hothouses," and "mountains of mirror." These images occur to the narrator because of the imaginative force of the name Glass House Mountains, but that same force also deprives her of the way she saw the mountains before they were named. The mountains now "form / in diamond panes behind the tree ferns of / the dark imagination." It is interesting that while glass is associated with light, the imagination is defined here as "dark." The "dark imagination," like the lush and fertile rain forest out of which the mountains rose, is mysterious; it contains more possibilities than Cook's naming does.

At the end of the poem the Glass House Mountains reflect "Cook upon a deck." Because Cook has made them glass, they will always reflect him--they are, indeed, "Cook's Mountains." In the final lines of the poem, Cook's tongue is "silvered" like a mirror--which may suggest that the name he gives to the mountains reflects them accurately. A silver tongue also indicates that one speaks well. But the tongue is "silvered with paradox and metaphor" because while language helps us to see in one way, it also keeps us from seeing in other ways. That is the paradox. The name is a metaphor: it stands for the mountains but is not identical with the mountains. Because the name takes over, substituting itself for the thing described, Cook in a sense takes possession of the mountains. This is why the poem is called "Cook's Mountains."

COMMENTS

The preceding explication focuses on the poem's theme of the paradoxical nature of language in general and of naming in particular. It is another A+ essay. There are obviously other interpretations the student could have pursued, and other details he could have chosen to support his interpretation. Certainly, he might have arrived a somewhat different sense of the balance between the positive and negative sides of the paradox, but a good essay would have to recognize that both sides exist. And it would have to do so even if the thesis didn't involve the paradox that is discussed at length in this essay. The idea of paradox is too big—too central to the poem's meaning—to leave out of your account altogether. Your own thesis might take you on a different path through the woods, but if you completely left out the basic idea contained in this explication you wouldn't even be in the same woods!

It's hard to predict what will strike any particular reader. Sometimes you get a lucky break. Say, for example, you studied Latin in high school and your teacher was always quoting Julius Caesar's famous line, "I came, I saw, I conquered." If that stuck in your memory, you might well hear an echo of it in the lines "[H]e came," "He saw," "They shone." That might cause you to develop the role of Cook as conqueror—and it works! Remember that one of the things explorers and conquerors do is to give new names to places. And there is indeed a historical and political subtext to this poem, since Captain Cook was one of the important forces behind the colonization of Australia. The fact that the poem is called "Cook's Mountains"—a title that signals Cook's desire to possess and "conquer"—and the fact that the named mountains "[reflect] Cook upon a deck" rather than the natural Australian landscape that surrounds them support this reading. In addition, you might have noticed the division between the stanzas: the first and last stanza are more objective and historical and there is no identified speaker, while the middle two stanzas tell a personal story about the experience the narrator and her companion had while travelling through Australia. The middle stanzas describe how Cook's vision imposed itself on their experience of the place. And the structure gives Cook both first and last word! Do you see how you might have developed an essay out of these thoughts?

Perhaps you are especially interested in or puzzled by the glass imagery in the poem, and would like to go further with that. If that is the case, you could, as I did on the marked-up copy of the poem, make a list of all the glass-related images and then think more about what they are doing there. You might want to talk about the how the mountains "broke / the light to fragments as the driver spoke." The fragments could certainly be shards of broken glass, but they could also indicate the fragmentation of the narrator, who, because the mountains have now been named, is forced to inhabit the paradoxical world of language. The expression "broke / the light to fragments" is a violent image; it reminds me of people saying that something "shattered their illusion." Our picture or our understanding of the world around us is as fragile and inflexible as glass: to change the way we understand the world requires a radical and violent shift in our perceptions. In connection with this analysis of the glass imagery, you might want to take a look at the lines "they form / in diamond panes behind the tree ferns of / the dark imagination." Diamonds are glasslike, but they are stronger than glass and can, in fact, *cut* glass. We might say that the diamond panes emphasize the hardness (and durability?) of the definition imposed on the mountains by the name Glass Mountains.

I'm just trying to get you started here. There are other interesting uses of the glass imagery that you might pursue as well. Taken together, these images are an important way of understanding what the poem is about; they are one obvious kind of path through the woods. You could say a lot of different things about this glass imagery. But you couldn't write a good explication of the poem without paying at least some attention to this central image pattern.

In explicating any poem, you will have to go into your own "dark imagination." What you come up with in the end will carry your own signature;

it will be at least a little different from what someone else might say. But it must respect the thing that is really there: the words on the page, as well as the mystery that is moving between the words—the mystery that the poet has tried to set in motion through words.

You might try thinking of a poem as an energy field, in which words have been selected and positioned with great care in order to set off certain vibrations in the reader. The poet's task is to take us *through* logic into the "dark imagination"; and your task, as critic, is to shed light on how the poet performs this magic.

HANDLING
QUOTATIONS AND
DOCUMENTATION

ACKNOWLEDGING SOURCES

There are two kinds of literary essays: those that analyze only the literary text that is the subject of your paper (the *primary* text) and those that *also* consider what others (in *secondary* texts) have said about the issues addressed in your essay. An English essay that relies heavily on secondary texts—the work of other critics, theoreticians, and literary historians—is sometimes called a research essay.

The *quotations* that you use in your essay may be from primary texts only or they may be from primary *and* secondary texts. Whenever you take material from a secondary text—whether it's a quotation or an idea—you must acknowledge your source. If you don't state where the passage or idea comes from, you are committing the very serious offence of *plagiarism*. Plagiarism is stealing. According to the *MLA Handbook* (1988), plagiarism involves "repeating someone else's particularly apt phrase without appropriate acknowledgement, paraphrasing another person's argument as your own, and presenting another's line of thinking as though it were your own." Plagiarism is a serious form of academic misconduct at most schools, and conviction of such an offence can lead to expulsion. If you are in doubt about whether or not to cite a source, cite it.

Quotations from Primary Texts

As I have repeatedly insisted, you must support your argument by referring to specific details from the primary text. Often it is best to present those details by direct quotation. The sample essay in this book illustrates how to cite passages from primary texts.

Lots of student writers have difficulty handling sources elegantly. For one thing, it's hard to know when to quote directly and when to paraphrase. Consider this: if you don't need the nuances of the author's language, it may be more efficient to use your own words.

Don't distort the original meaning of the passage. You don't have to copy a whole passage if all you really need is a small part of it, but don't cut out things that are inconvenient because they weaken your argument. And don't quote the writer out of context. Be fair.

Be selective about what you quote. If the passage is not entirely relevant to your point, don't use it. Be wary of using too many quotations. Essays that consist of a series of quotations loosely strung together are not acceptable. Remember that your instructor is mainly interested in what *you* have to say about the material.

Your goal is to incorporate the quoted material as smoothly as possible into your own writing. Poorly integrated quotations make your essay choppy and fragmented. Well-integrated quotations maintain the flow of your own writing. *Study Version 4 of the sample essay to see how quotations can be worked into your essay.*

Research Papers

Much of what I have said above applies to quotations from secondary sources as well: don't distort, and be selective. Use secondary sources to *support* your argument, not to *replace* it. Often students become intimidated by the critics and decide that only the critics' opinions on a text can be right. Have some faith in your own critical intelligence. You may well find that what the critics have to say alters your perspective, but don't assume you're wrong! Lots of foolish ideas have made their way into print. Besides, any powerful literary text can sustain more than one interpretation. Use a particular critic only if she (or he) gave you the idea, or if she says something more effectively than you possibly can say it, or if you disagree with her. Don't be afraid to disagree. Some of the best essays I have read involve a student's rejection or modification of a critic's opinion.

Punctuation and Page References

If a page reference is given after the quotation, the punctuation follows the page reference.

"The dog is dead" (8).

"The dog is dead" (8), but the cat seems to be doing fine.

If the *quotation* ends with an exclamation point or question mark, but your sentence doesn't, handle it this way:

The narrator's alarm is apparent: "Is the dog dead?" (9).

If you are quoting repeatedly from the same page, you can decide not to provide a page reference after each quotation. Instead, just give the page reference after the last quotation in the series. Remember that wherever you *don't* give a page reference, the punctuation goes *inside* the quotation marks.

The heroine is "fairly quiet," has "smouldering eyes," and is "as slim as a young birch" (12).

Here are a few rules concerning the mechanics of using quotations—how to introduce them, how to present them, and how to reference them.

SHORT PROSE QUOTATIONS

Short quotations of four typed lines or fewer are best integrated into your own sentence.

Enclose the quoted passage within double quotation marks and put the page reference before the period. If you quote dialogue or something else that is already in quotation marks, you must put single quotation marks inside the double ones.

The narrator places himself within a specific spatial location where even the house in which he lives "has its own topography, its own lore: negotiable borders, spaces open or closed, the salient features—not Capes and Bays in this case but the Side Door, the Brass Jardiniere—whose names make up a daily litany" (9).

For focus and economy, you may integrate the quoted passage into your own discussion to underline salient parts of the quotation.

original passage: "Her skin had a pattern all its own of numberless branching wrinkles and as though a whole little tree stood in the middle of her forehead, but a golden color ran underneath, and the two knobs of her cheeks were illumined by a yellow burning under the dark" (8).

integrated quotation: Welty paints in Phoenix's face a landscape of ripeness and love, with "numberless branching wrinkles" and a "golden color" (8).

If you can't make the passage fit into your own sentence, introduce it with a colon. Remember, though, that the part of the sentence that comes before the colon must be an *independent* clause (with a subject and a verb).

Phoenix's wrinkled face is as time-worn as old as the path upon which she walks. The wrinkles are also branches of a tree, signalling her participation in nature: "[h]er skin had a pattern all its own of numberless branching wrinkles and as though a whole little tree stood in the middle of her forehead . . ." (8).

Note in the example above that I have not quoted the whole sentence. You may choose to omit parts of the sentence, but you must mark the place where something is left out with an ellipsis (three spaced periods).

You may make small changes to individual words, but you must mark those changes by putting them in square brackets. In the example above, I have changed the "H" of the original to lowercase to be consistent with the grammar of my sentence. Sometimes you may wish to clarify a pronoun by inserting the name of the character to whom it refers enclosed within square brackets.

"The child knew that she [Elaine] could save her."

LONG PROSE QUOTATIONS

A long quotation is more than four typed lines. Remember to avoid copying large amounts of original text as filler. Before you include it, consider whether a long quotation is necessary to your point.

1. Double-space the quoted passage.
2. In most cases, introduce the passage with a colon.
3. Indent the whole passage ten spaces from the left margin as a block quotation. If the passage either begins a new paragraph or includes a new paragraph, indent the new paragraph line an additional three spaces.
4. The indentation of a block quotation is equivalent to putting it in quotation marks, so you don't need quotation marks *except* when your

quoted material includes dialogue.

5. Put the period at the end of the quoted passage, leave two spaces, and then put the page reference in parentheses after the period.

example of block quotation:

The narrator emphasizes the precariousness and danger of his father's position by juxtaposing the house and the money that bought the house (the ultimate signs of civilization) to the natural environment:

> And nature advanced. Tea bush became jungle, branches put their arms into the windows. If you stood still you were invaded. Wealth that was static quickly rotted. The paper money in your pocket, wet from your own sweat gathered mould. (189)

The landscape enters and threatens the human space of the home.

VERSE QUOTATIONS

Verse quotations are handled in the same way as prose quotations. Remember to reproduce the original faithfully, including all internal punctuation and capital letters. It is also important—particularly in contemporary poetry—to reproduce the spatial arrangement of the original as exactly as possible.

1. Rather than page references, cite line numbers. If your source is a play, give act, scene, and line numbers in that order.
2. You may omit several lines of verse, but you must indicate that something is missing by typing in a line of spaced periods.
3. If you are quoting up to three lines of a poem or play, the quotation should be incorporated into your writing. Use the virgule (slash), with a space before and after it, to indicate where the line breaks.

The hawk is totally self-centred and supremely confident: "It took the whole of Creation / To produce my foot, my each feather: / Now I hold Creation in my feet" (8–10).

Note that the capital letter at the beginning of each line is retained, as is the internal punctuation.

4. Longer quotations should be set off as you would set off a block prose quotation. If the line is too long to accommodate a ten-space indenta-

tion, you may indent fewer spaces.

example of block verse quotation:

Hamlet exalts his father by comparing his features to those of classical gods:

> See what a grace was seated on this brow:
> Hyperion's curls, the front of Jove himself,
> An eye like Mars, to threaten and command,
> A station like the herald Mercury
> New-lighted on a heaven-kissing hill—
> A combination and a form indeed
> Where every god did seem to set his seal,
> To give the world assurance of a man. (3.4.56–63)

With these words he hopes to remind his mother that the husband she lost was a man of extraordinary quality.

QUOTATIONS FROM SECONDARY SOURCES

Remember that all borrowings from secondary sources must be documented. Basically you integrate a passage from a critical source in the way you would handle a quotation from a novel or a poem. But there are a few more things to think about.

The *MLA Handbook for Writers of Research Papers,* third edition, is a standard reference text. It recommends a simple and straightforward documentation system that eliminates the need for footnotes or endnotes. The author's name and the page reference are placed within the text of your essay, and the full bibliographic citation is given on a separate "Works Cited" page.

Note: For some essays you may feel a need to provide a "Notes" page. Generally, these pages enable you to give information that is relevant to your argument but that will cause a bit of a detour in its logic. Say, for example, you cited a critic in your essay and wanted to refer the reader to other critics who were pursuing the same idea or issue. In that case, you would put a footnote number after your analysis of the critic's ideas. Then on the "Notes" page you would create an entry with the corresponding number that might look like this:

1. See also Hutcheon (1992); Murray (1988); Bennett (1994).

The references to Hutcheon, Murray, and Bennett would be included in your "Works Cited."

You might also want to provide information that is interesting but tangential to your argument, like some relevant biographical information on an author, or a brief acknowledgment (for the purpose of fairness) of the context of, or other dimensions of, a critic's argument. By making an annotation like this, you maintain the flow of your essay, and the reader can choose whether to stop and read the endnote, or to read it later.

Documenting Secondary Sources

The parenthetical reference that follows the quotation in your main text must correspond with a citation on the "Works Cited" page so that the reader can quickly look up the source.

1. Book by a single author

There are two ways of referencing the source:

a. Put the author's last name and the page number in parentheses.
b. Incorporate the author's name (and possibly even the title of the book) into your prose, giving only the page number in parentheses.

Method 1: Time, and in particular past time, is an important motif in Mavis Gallant's fiction. In fact, one could say that "Gallant's stories have developed and sustained her exploration of the past as time misapprehended" (Besner 117).

Method 2: In fact, as Besner notes in his book *The Light of Imagination: Mavis Gallant's Fiction,* "Gallant's stories have developed and sustained her exploration of the past as time misapprehended" (117).

If two books by the same author are quoted, put an abbreviated version of the title after the author's name in the parenthetical reference—e.g., "(Besner, *Light* 117)"—so that it is clear which work your quotation is taken from.

2. Book by more than one author

In general, list each of the authors' last names in the parenthetical reference. If there are more than three, you may state the first author's name and then put "et al."

Language, "shifty, tricky, quicksilver stuff" (Dean, Gibson, Wilson 27), cannot be contained in dictionaries.

3. Article by a single author

Document an article in the same way as a book. Remember not to duplicate information. If you put the author's name in your main text, do not include it in the parenthetical reference.

> Murphy suggests that the Captain-narrator in "The Secret Sharer" is an unreliable narrator (193).

> Another critic notes Eliot's tendency to repeat specific motifs and images in order to create unique patterns of meaning (Scofield 5).

WORKS CITED

All the information you need can usually be found on the copyright page of a book or on the first page of a journal. The "Works Cited" page belongs at the end of your essay.

1. Centre the title (Works Cited), but don't put it in all capital letters; enclose it within quotation marks, or underline it.
2. Double-space within and between each entry.
3. Begin each entry at the left margin, but indent all subsequent lines five spaces.
4. List entries alphabetically by author's last name. If the author's name is unknown, alphabetize the first letter of the title—excluding "A," "An," or "The."

Standard Format

The two examples below represent the standard citation format for a book and for a journal article. Other examples of how to cite different kinds of sources follow.

1. Book

> Besner, Neil K. *The Light of Imagination: Mavis Gallant's Fiction.* Vancouver: U of British Columbia P, 1988.

2. Journal article

> Everett, Barbara. "In Search of Prufrock." *Critical Quarterly* 16.2 (1974): 101–21.

Note: Include issue number only for a journal with noncontinuous pagination.

MORE SAMPLE 'WORKS CITED' CITATIONS

Books

1. More than one book by the same author

You don't have to repeat the author's name. Just type three hyphens followed by a period instead of the name and alphabetize the entries according to the first letter of the title.

> Atwood, Margaret. *Cat's Eye.* Toronto: McClelland & Stewart, 1988.

> – – –. *The Handmaid's Tale.* Toronto: McClelland & Stewart, 1985.

2. Book by more than one author

List the names, separated by commas and a final "and" as they appear on the title page. Reverse only the first name. If there are more than three authors, you may state the first name and add "et al."

> Dean, Leonard F., Walker Gibson, and Kenneth G. Wilson. *The Play of Language.* New York: Oxford UP, 1971.

> Dickenson, J.P., et al. *A Geography of the Third World.* London: Methuen, 1983.

3. An anthology

Use this format if you wish to cite the *entire* book.

> Neuman, Shirley, and Smaro Kamboureli, eds. *A Mazing Space: Writing Canadian Women Writing.* Edmonton: Longspoon/NeWest Press, 1986.

4. A work in an anthology

Use this format if you want to cite something that is *in* the anthology. Be sure to include the page numbers of the piece you are citing.

> Blaise, Clark. "To Begin, To Begin." *Reading Our World: The Guelph*

Anthology. Eds. Constance Rooke, Renée Hulan, and Linda Warley. Needham Heights: Ginn, 1990. 1–4.

5. An edition that is not the first

Many books are published in more than one edition, and, since changes are made in the revising of editions, it's important to identify which edition you have used. It could be a numbered edition, a revised edition, or an edition published for a specific country, e.g., a Canadian edition. This information should be abbreviated and placed immediately after the title. The publication place and date you give *must* be for the edition you have used.

> Corder, Jim W., and Walter S. Avis. *Handbook of Current English.* Canadian ed. Toronto: Gage, 1979.

> Clough, Shepard B., et al. *European History in a World Perspective.* 3rd ed. Lexington: D.C. Heath, 1975.

6. A republished book

Many books, particularly works of fiction, are published in different versions (hardcover or paperback) or by different publishers. So it's important to identify the particular book you have used. Put the *original* publication date after the title and before the publication information for the book you have used.

> Atwood, Margaret. *The Handmaid's Tale.* 1985. Toronto: Bantam, 1986.

7. A book that is part of a series

If the title page indicates that the book is part of a publisher's series, include the series title (not underlined) and number (if there is one) before the publication information. Abbreviate series (ser.) if it is part of the name.

> Cameron, Barry. *John Metcalf.* Twayne's World Authors Ser. 771. Boston: Twayne, 1986.

> Daiches, David. "The Poetry of Dylan Thomas." *Dylan Thomas: A Collection of Critical Essays.* Ed. C.B. Cox. Twentieth Century Views. Englewood Cliffs, NJ: Prentice-Hall, 1966. 14–24.

8. A work from a book that is part of a multivolume work

If you used only one volume of a multivolume work, you must indicate which volume you used. If the volume has its own title, include the volume title after the author's name. Cite the title of the whole series before the publication information. If you cite only a part of a volume, include the inclusive page numbers after the publication date.

> Eliot, T.S. "The Waste Land." *The Norton Anthology of American Literature.* Eds. Nina Byam et al. 3rd ed. Vol. 2. New York: Norton, 1989. 1278–91.

> "Rhys, Jean." *Contemporary Authors.* Ed. Christine Nasso. Rev. ed. Vols. 25–28. Detroit: Gale Research, 1977. 588–89.

Periodicals

1. Article from a journal with continuous pagination

Some journals continue page numbers from issue to issue so that one whole volume has consecutive numbering. If you are citing an article from one of these journals, omit the issue number before the date. Note that there are no periods either after the journal title or before the parentheses.

> Sharpe, Jenny. "Figures of Colonial Resistance." *Modern Fiction Studies* 35 (1989): 137–55.

2. Article from a journal with noncontinuous pagination

If each issue is numbered separately, include the issue number after the volume number (put a period but no space in between).

> Brydon, Diana. "Troppo Agitato: Writing and Reading Cultures." *Ariel* 19.1 (1988): 13–21.

Sometimes two issues are combined; in that case, cite both numbers.

> Levitt, Morton. "Regional, National, and Ethnic Literatures: Annual Review." *Journal of Modern Literature* 17.2–3. (1990): 253–81.

3. Work from a magazine published weekly

Omit "The" from the title. Do not put a period between the magazine title and the date. Cite the complete date in the order day, month (abbreviated), year.

> Munro, Alice. "Friend of My Youth." *New Yorker* 22 Jan. 1990: 36–48.

4. Article from a magazine published monthly

Cite only the month (abbreviated) and the year.

> Glendinning, Victoria. "Lady Oracle." *Saturday Night* Jan. 1986.

5. Article from a newspaper

Omit "The" from the title of the newspaper. Cite the complete date (day, abbreviated month, year) and the section and page number.

> Kirchoff, H.J. "When Print Meets Oral Culture." *Globe and Mail* 30 Sept. 1989: C10.

6. Book review

Begin the citation with the reviewer's name and the title of the review. Then put "Rev. of" and the title of the book reviewed, a comma, the word "by" and the author of the book. Complete the citation as normal.

> Fitzgerald, Judith. "A Necessary Allegory." Rev. of *The Handmaid's Tale,* by Margaret Atwood. *Canadian Forum* Oct. 1985: 30–31.

7. Interview

Begin with the name of the person interviewed. Then cite the title of the interview, or, if there is none, write the word "Interview." You may include the name of the interviewer introduced by the word "By." Complete the citation as normal.

> Atwood, Margaret. Interview. By Geoff Hancock. *Canadian Fiction Magazine* 58 (1986): 113–44.

> Kroetsch, Robert. "Uncovering Our Dream World: An Interview with Robert Kroetsch." By Robert Enright and Dennis Cooley. *Essays in Canadian Writing* 18–19 (1980): 21–32.

A QUICK GUIDE TO GRAMMAR AND PUNCTUATION

This guide offers a summary of the basic rules of grammar and punctuation. They are the conventions you should follow when writing a formal academic essay. I'll begin by defining the parts of speech and the parts of a sentence, which you need to understand in order to understand the rules.

PARTS OF SPEECH

Nouns

Nouns can be classified in a number of ways. They can be proper—that is, they can name specific people, places, or things—or common; they can also be concrete or abstract, singular or plural, collective, or possessive. Nouns can have several functions in a sentence, but remember that any noun can be the subject of a sentence. If you're trying to figure out whether a word is a noun, ask yourself whether it can be followed by a verb. (For example: Mary *is* . . ., Comedies *are* . . ., Happiness *depends* . . .)

Proper Nouns

Names of people are always capitalized.

> **Enzo Careri is a good student.**
> **My best friend is Melissa Talbot.**

Titles of people: A title should be capitalized if it is used as part of a person's name, but not if it is used as a descriptive term.

Professor Lancashire teaches poetry.
Amanda Lancashire is a professor who teaches poetry.

Names of groups—racial, linguistic, religious, or political groups—are always capitalized.

The Blacks in South Africa finally have the right to vote in federal elections.
I live in an Italian neighbourhood in Toronto.
My father used to be a Liberal, but now he is a New Democrat.

Names of organizations—like associations, clubs, and political groups—are capitalized.

I belong to the Modern Language Association.
The Girl Guides of Canada sell cookies to raise money.

Place names are capitalized.

Three of the students in my class are from Portugal.
Banff National Park is a great place to go hiking.
The intersection of Portage and Main is legendary.

Note: Capitalize directions only when they are part of the place name, as opposed to a general geographic area.

Many explorers spent time looking for the Northwest Passage.
My brother lives in Northern Ontario.

Names of institutions are capitalized.

I used to be a librarian at the St. John's Public Library.
The University of Victoria has a beautiful campus.

Note: Don't capitalize institutions unless the name of a specific institution is given.

The town council recently approved funding for a public library.
The Eramosa Town Council recently approved funding for a public library.
I would like to attend a well-established university.
The University of Toronto is a well-established university.

Common Nouns

Common nouns name nonspecific people, places, or things. Common nouns are not capitalized.

> The *woman* who did a guest *lecture* in our *class* was very informative.
> My *children* like to go to the *beach.*
> My *car* has overheated.

- *Concrete nouns* name things that can be seen or touched.

  > My *computer* is down.
  > The *coffee* is in the *pot.*

- *Abstract nouns* name a condition, quality, action, or idea.

  > Many doctors are interested in the *causes* of *senility.*
  > I think Canadians take their *freedom* for granted.

- Most nouns have a *singular* and a *plural* form.

  > *singular:* The *cyclist* is lobbying for a bike *lane.*
  > *plural:*   Most *cyclists* believe that every city should have bike *lanes.*
  > *singular:* A *wolf* was seen in the forest.
  > *plural:*   *Wolves* are a threat to livestock.

- *Collective nouns* name groups of individuals.

  > My family is very important to me.
  > The crowd cheered when the band started playing.

- *Possessive nouns* show ownership and are always followed by another noun.

  > The *minister's* son plays on my basketball team.
  > The *professor's* notes have been misplaced.

Pronouns

Pronouns are words that take the place of nouns. The specific noun that a pronoun replaces is its *antecedent.*

> The main character in *The Stone Angel* is Hagar Shipley. She is an old woman reflecting on her life.

Here the pronoun *she* stands in for the noun Hagar Shipley; Hagar Shipley is the antecedent.

- *Personal pronouns* substitute for particular people or things *(I, she, him, we, them).*

- *Possessive pronouns* show ownership. Unlike possessive nouns—for example, *Charley's* aunt—possessive pronouns do not take an apostrophe *(my, his, mine, our, theirs).*

- *Relative pronouns*—words like *who, whom, that,* and *which*—begin what are called adjective clauses; these are groups of words that look something like a sentence, since they have a subject and a verb, but they act like an adjective and modify nouns and pronouns.

    The man who is the benefactor is a convict.
    My grandmother, whom I adore, is coming to stay for a week.
    In the Skin of a Lion, which I have read eleven times, is one of my favourite books.

Note: *That* introduces a restrictive clause, while *which* introduces a nonrestrictive clause. Restrictive clauses contain information that is crucial to the meaning of the sentence, while nonrestrictive clauses contain information that is helpful but not essential.

    The performance of Hamlet that I saw last week was spectacular.
    Hamlet's soliloquy, which is one of the most moving speeches in literature, is found in Act III.

- *Interrogative pronouns* are, in many cases, the same words as relative pronouns. As interrogative pronouns, however, words like *who, whom, which, what,* and *whose* begin questions.

    What is the title of Margaret Laurence's first novel?
    Which novel shall I give my brother for his birthday?
    Whose glasses are these on the table?

Note: The case of an interrogative pronoun—that is, whether to use *who* or *whom*—depends on its function in the sentence.

    Who were Anne's kindred spirits in Anne of Green Gables?
    Whom do you prefer to read, Rudy Wiebe or Alice Munro?

- *Indefinite pronouns* indicate nonspecific groups of people or things *(anyone, everyone, each, either, several, some, nobody)*.

- *Intensive pronouns* are used for emphasis; they emphasize nouns or other pronouns.

  The chef *herself* came to ask if we had enjoyed our dinner.

- *Reflexive pronouns* indicate that the receiver of the action and the doer of the action are one and the same.

  I dared *myself* to do it.

Verbs

Verbs express action or a state of being. Every sentence contains at least one main verb, and often an auxiliary or helping verb is attached to a main verb.

I *write* my last exam today.

Here *write* is the main verb.

He *has* not *expressed* his opinion.

Here *has* is the helping verb and *expressed* is the main verb.

Luke *loved* and *left* Laura.

Here *loved* and *left* are the main verbs of the sentence.

Adjectives

Adjectives are modifiers. They describe nouns or pronouns (the *main* character, my *youngest* sister). They usually go before the noun they describe (*broken* heart, *rhyming* couplet), although sometimes they go after a linking verb and describe the subject (The cat is *striped*. The ending is *surprising*).

Adverbs

Adverbs are modifiers too; but, unlike adjectives, they modify verbs, adjectives, and other adverbs. They often end in *ly*.

Abdul read *quickly*.

Here *quickly* modifies the verb *read*.

The *really* poignant story won the prize.

Here *really* modifies the adjective *poignant.*

Vladimir spoke *somewhat* skeptically about the deal.

Here *somewhat* modifies the adverb *skeptically.*

Prepositions

Prepositions are words *(on, of, under, between, before)* that usually precede a noun or a pronoun and that introduce a prepositional phrase. The noun in the prepositional phrase is called the object of the preposition.

On the chair

Here *on* is the preposition that begins the prepositional phrase, and *chair* is the object of the preposition.

in whatever style he liked

Here *in* is the preposition and *whatever style he liked* is a noun clause acting as the object of the preposition.

Conjunctions

Conjunctions are words that demonstrate the relationship between parts of the sentence; they can occur between words, phrases, or clauses.

Conjunctions can be *coordinating*, which means that they join grammatically equal elements of the sentence *(and, yet, but). Correlative* conjunctions are always found in pairs and they join grammatically parallel elements *(not only . . . but also, neither . . . nor). Subordinating conjunctions* introduce subordinate clauses *(although, because, unless)*, while *conjunctive adverbs* indicate the relation between two independent clauses *(therefore, furthermore, nevertheless).*

Interjections

Interjections are used to show surprise.

Wow!
Alas!

PARTS OF A SENTENCE

Subjects and Predicates

The two basic grammatical parts of the sentence are the *subject* and the *predicate*. The *subject* of a sentence, which names who or what the sentence is about, includes the simple subject and all of the words associated with it.

The prologue of Ishiguro's novel describes the setting of the story.

The word *prologue* is the simple subject, while *The prologue of Ishiguro's novel* is the complete subject.

The *predicate* of a sentence includes the verb, which expresses action or being, and all of the words associated with it.

Offred, the heroine of Atwood's *The Handmaid's Tale*, remembers what her life was like before the revolution.

The word *remembers* is the verb, while *remembers what her life was like before the revolution* is the complete predicate.

Phrases and Clauses

A *phrase* is a group of words that doesn't have a subject and a verb.

down a worn path
to the doctor's office

A *clause* is a group of words containing both a subject and a verb.

when Phoenix meets the hunter

The subject is *Phoenix* and the verb is *meets*. The word *when* is a signal of dependence. It tells you that what you have here is a dependent clause.

Phoenix walks

The subject is *Phoenix* and the verb is *walks*. There is no signal of dependence, so this clause is an independent clause.

Dependent and Independent Clauses

There are two kinds of clauses: independent and dependent (or subordinate). An *independent clause* can stand alone as a complete sentence. In fact, the minimum requirement of a sentence is one independent clause.

The ending is surprising.
Homosexuality is a human rights issue.

A *dependent clause* cannot be a complete sentence. It has the same grammatical function as a single word: adverb, adjective, or noun. There are three kinds of dependent clauses: adverb, adjective, and noun.

- *Adverb clauses* can modify verbs, adjectives, or other adverbs. They begin with signals of dependence called *subordinate conjunctions,* words such as *because, unless, since, as, when, where, if, although, before, whether, while, why, after, as soon as, even though, in case, than, that, until, what, whatever, whenever, whereas,* and *wherever.*
  Here's an adverb clause modifying a verb:

  The poems were written *when Keats was a young man.*

  The adverb clause *when Keats was a young man* modifies the verb *written.*
  Here's an adverb clause modifying an adjective:

  Keats was an excellent poet *when he was young.*

  Here the adverb clause *when he was young* modifies the adjective *excellent.*
  And here's an adverb clause modifying an adverb:

  Keats wrote the poems quickly *because he was inspired.*

  Here the adverb clause *because he was inspired* modifies the adverb *quickly.*

- *Adjective clauses* modify nouns or pronouns. They begin with *relative pronouns*—words like *who, whose, whom, which* and *that.*

  Shakespeare, *who lived during the Elizabethan period,* wrote plays of great moral complexity.

- *Noun clauses* function as nouns. They can be either the subject of a sentence or the object of a verb or a preposition. The signals of dependence for noun clauses are words like *that, whoever, whichever, who, what, how, why, when* and *where.*

Here's a noun clause functioning as the subject:

That Phoenix has had a hard life is never in doubt.

Here's a noun clause that is the object of the verb:

P.K. Page showed *that it is difficult to be an only child.*

And here's a noun clause that is the object of a preposition:

She wrote poems about *whatever struck her fancy.*

Restrictive and Nonrestrictive Clauses

Adjective and adverb clauses may be restrictive or nonrestrictive. A restrictive clause is one that *restricts* or limits the meaning of the thing it modifies. A nonrestrictive clause simply gives extra, nonessential information. *Note carefully:* Nonrestrictive clauses are set off by commas on both sides; restrictive clauses are *not* set off (see the section on commas, pages 90–93).

- Here is a *restrictive adjective clause:*

The poems *that describe her children* are filled with maternal images.

This clause *restricts* the meaning of the sentence, since only the poems that describe her children have maternal images.

- Here is a *nonrestrictive adjective clause:*

These poems, *which he wrote when he was very young,* are heavily ironic.

The main idea is that these poems are heavily ironic; the information given in the adjective clause is not essential.

Fragments

A fragment is anything written as a sentence that is less than a complete sentence. In other words, it begins with a capital letter and ends with a period, but it is not a sentence. Remember that a sentence must have at least one independent clause. Most fragment errors fall into two kinds:

- A dependent clause is written as if it were a sentence.

> **wrong:**   While the detective carried out his investigation.

Here, the signal of dependence *while* tells you that this is a dependent clause, not a proper sentence.

> **correct:**   While the detective carried out his investigation, we looked for clues.

- A verbal is confused with a proper verb. Verbals are words formed from verbs. But they are *not verbs!* There are three kinds of verbals: infinitives (*to* + verb), gerunds (verb + *ing*), and participles (verb + *ing*, verb + *ed*, or *having* + past tense). Gerunds and present participles look alike but have different grammatical functions. Gerunds act as nouns; participles act as adjectives.

Here are some fragments caused by confusing a verbal with a proper verb:

> **wrong:**   The lawyer *being* certain that his client was innocent.
> **correct:**   The lawyer was certain that his client was innocent.

> **wrong:**   To run like a champion.
> **correct:**   She runs like a champion.

Joining Independent Clauses

Independent clauses can be joined in three ways:

- The *comma and* construction

The book is written in dialect, and it has a first-person narrator.

The coordinating conjunction *and*, preceded by the *comma*, correctly joins two independent clauses. Don't forget the comma.

There are seven coordinating conjunctions—*and, but, or, nor, so, for* and *yet*—and all can be used together with a comma to join two or more independent clauses.

- The semicolon

You can also join independent clauses with a semicolon. This method works particularly well when the clauses are contrasted.

Earl steals cars; Edna goes along for the ride.

If the logical relationship between the two clauses is clear, all you need is the semicolon. But if the connection between the clauses needs some clarification, use the semicolon together with a *conjunctive adverb*, words like *therefore, however, furthermore, accordingly, also, otherwise, likewise, nevertheless, consequently, all the same, at the same time, besides, conversely, for that reason, hence, however, in fact, indeed, moreover, on the contrary, on the other hand, rather, still, then, thus.*

Atwood's fictional handmaids wear red; thus, they are associated with fertility.

You can also use a semicolon (instead of a comma) with a coordinating conjunction. This marks a clear division between the independent clauses when they contain other commas.

Glenn Gould, who was one of Canada's most inspired pianists, died an early death; yet, thanks to recording technology, his work survives on tapes and compact discs.

- The colon

Use the colon to join independent clauses when the second clause is introduced by or completes the thought of the first.

Adam Bede is sure of one thing: he loves Hetty.

Joining Multiple Independent Clauses

If your sentence has *more than two* independent clauses, the same rules apply. The semicolon is a conspicuous mark of punctuation. If you use it, you're signalling that this is the logical middle of the sentence.

Offred loves Luke, and she wants him back; nevertheless, she begins to love Nick.

Notice there are three independent clauses in this sentence. The semicolon goes between the half of the sentence on Luke and the half on Nick.

If you have three or more parts of the sentence all of equal weight, then use the same mark of punctuation between each.

The tone is bitter, the language is harsh, and the images are apocalyptic.

Barbara, who is very shy, loves Roy, the man from Montreal; Roy loves the ambitious one, Angela; and Terry is in love with Barbara.

Here semicolons are used because of the internal use of commas.

Run-On Sentences and Comma Splices

Run-ons and comma splices result from the failure to join independent clauses correctly.

- A *run-on sentence* is one in which two or more independent clauses have been run together. (Note: A run-on sentence is *not* just a sentence that runs on too long.)

  wrong: **Shakespeare's sonnets are witty Keats's are not.**
  correct: **Shakespeare's sonnets are witty; Keats's are not.**

- A *comma splice* results when two independent clauses have been spliced together with *only* a comma. Sometimes the coordinating conjunction has been omitted.

  wrong: **Mordechai hates Algebra, Ruth hates English.**
  correct: **Mordechai hates Algebra, and Ruth hates English.**

Sometimes a comma is used where a semicolon is required. (A semicolon is required before a conjunctive adverb.)

  wrong: **John puts all of his time and energy into the company, however,**
              when promotions come up, he is passed by.
  correct: **John puts all of his time and energy into the company; however,**
              when promotions come up, he is passed by.

PUNCTUATION

Punctuation is important for clarity; if you use incorrect punctuation, you may obscure the meaning of your sentence. You may also interfere with the flow of your sentence. I have taken the first paragraph of Margaret Laurence's *The*

Diviners and altered the original punctuation to show how important it is to punctuate correctly.

> The river flowed, both ways. The current moved from north, to south but the wind usually came from the south rippling, the bronze-green water in the opposite, direction. This apparently impossible, contradiction made apparent, and possible still fascinated Morag, even, after years of river-watching.

Now I have provided the original paragraph so you can see how beautifully the writing flows, and how clear the meaning of the paragraph is.

> The river flowed both ways. The current moved from north to south, but the wind usually came from the south, rippling the bronze-green water in the opposite direction. This apparently impossible contradiction, made apparent and possible, still fascinated Morag, even after years of river-watching.

Commas

The Comma and Construction

The comma is used in the *comma and* construction to join independent clauses. The conjunctions that can be used to join independent clauses are *and, but, or, nor, so, for,* and *yet.* Don't forget the comma.

> The images of hunger are disturbing, yet they are also strangely beautiful.

The Intrusive Comma Error

An intrusive comma is one that *intrudes* or places a barrier between two things that should not be separated.

- A comma separating a subject from its verb is incorrect.

  wrong: Stealing the car, leads to Earl's downfall.
  correct: Stealing the car leads to Earl's downfall.

- A comma that intrudes between a verb and its object is also wrong.

  wrong: John Agard wrote, "The Palm Tree King."
  correct: John Agard wrote "The Palm Tree King."

- A comma inserted between the last adjective in a series and the noun it modifies is intrusive.

| *wrong:* | Rhys is a poetic, visionary, writer. |
| *correct:* | Rhys is a poetic, visionary writer. |

You should also beware of the intrusive comma between pairs of words joined by a coordinating conjunction. These pairs are found in compound subjects, compound verbs, and compound objects.

| *wrong:* | Margaret Atwood, and Margaret Laurence are both Canadian writers. |
| *correct:* | Margaret Atwood and Margaret Laurence are both Canadian writers. |

| *wrong:* | The ball bounced, and rolled. |
| *correct:* | The ball bounced and rolled. |

| *wrong:* | Shakespeare wrote poems, and plays. |
| *correct:* | Shakespeare wrote poems and plays. |

A Comma for Easier Reading

A comma can sometimes be used between parallel elements, especially when these elements are *long* or *contrasted*. This is technically an optional comma, but you should use it if it makes your sentence easier to read.

The farmer told her husband that the land, which she had farmed for many generations and which she loved, was no longer fertile, and that they would have to move.

Here, the comma separates parallel noun clauses ("that the land . . ." and "that they would . . .").

Phoenix sees things not because she is senile, but because she has a strong imagination.

The comma is a good idea here because it marks the contrast between the two parallel elements.

Serial Commas

Put commas between items in a series. You need a comma between the *and* and the last item.

The film starred Warren Beatty, Al Pacino, and Madonna.
The dog barked madly, swung in a circle, and pulled on its leash.

Commas between Coordinate Adjectives

Adjectives that are coordinate (equal in value) must be separated by commas.

Blood Relations is a provocative, brilliant play.

Sometimes an adjective is so closely bound to the noun it modifies that we think of it as part of the noun. In these cases, any other adjective that you might use with it is not coordinate, and you would not put a comma between the adjectives.

The singer was wearing a black leather jacket.

Since the adjective leather seems to be part of the noun *jacket, black* and *leather* are not coordinate, and you wouldn't put a comma between them.

The simplest way to determine whether adjectives are coordinate is to see if they can be joined by the word *and*. If you could use *and*, the adjectives are coordinate. You could say "provocative and brilliant play," but you wouldn't say "black and leather jacket."

Commas to Set Off

Elements in sentences (words, phrases, or clauses) that you choose to set off must be set off on *both* sides by a *pair* of commas. Dependent clauses, appositives, and participial phrases are set off only when they are *nonrestrictive* (i.e., when they are not essential to the meaning of the sentence).

My father, an enthusiastic gardener, is president of the Horticultural Society.

An appositive is a noun or a noun phrase that is found close to another noun and that supplements its meaning by describing or identifying it. The appositive here—*an enthusiastic gardener*—is set off on both sides because it gives additional (nonessential) information.

Atwood's novel *The Handmaid's Tale* is set in the near future.

Here, the appositive *(The Handmaid's Tale)* is not set off because it restricts the meaning of *novel*. Without the appositive, we wouldn't know which of Atwood's novels was meant.

The handsome man sat in the corner, sipping coffee and reading the newspaper.

The participial phrase is nonrestrictive. (The period takes the place of the second comma.)

The woman wearing the red hat is Clarissa.

Here, the participial phrase is not set off because it limits or restricts the meaning of *woman*.
Introductory phrases and clauses are often set off.

On the other hand, her character is less rebellious than others.
Before reading the story, consider these questions.

Interrupters are set off.

The book has not, I surmise, been properly edited.

Semicolons

There are only two possible uses of the semicolon.

- Semicolons join independent clauses—with or without a conjunctive adverb.

  He wants to remain friends with Bimbo; however, Jimmy's ego gets in the way.
  Amelia loved the book; I hated it.

- Semicolons can also be used to separate internally punctuated elements in a series. This second use of the semicolon is not common. Remember that in all other cases, you must have an independent clause on each side of the semicolon.

  Anne saw that the company's sales were lagging; feared—despite confident predictions from the marketing department—that the situation would not improve; and, when their competitor made her an offer, quit her job.

Colons

A colon is used when the first part of a sentence introduces or announces the second part. The colon must be *preceded* by an independent clause. What follows it, however, may be an independent clause, a phrase, a list, or a quotation.

One thought kept her going: Mayday might come to her rescue.

correct: **The main characters are the following: Lily, Kate, and Turner.**
better: **The main characters are Lily, Kate, and Turner.**

(Notice that you can't say "The main characters are: Lily, Kate, and Turner," because you must have a complete statement—an independent clause—before the colon.)

Dashes and Parentheses

Dashes or parentheses may be used to set off parenthetic elements. Generally, though, use commas to set off unless you have a good reason to prefer either dashes or parentheses.

Use dashes to set off abrupt interrupters or parts of the sentence to which you wish to draw attention.

Darren—known for his quick play—won the game for Barrytown.
The environmentalist's slogan—reduce, reuse, and recycle—has entered the popular consciousness.

Because the parenthetic element in the second example contains internal commas, the dashes are preferable to commas.

Use parentheses when you wish to de-emphasize the parenthetic element.

Ondaatje (a Canadian born in Sri Lanka) won the Booker Prize.

A single dash is often used if the element to be set off comes at the end of a sentence.

Judy was determined to get to Jamaica—even if she had to swim!

(The exclamation point replaces the second dash.)
Don't mix and match, using one dash and one comma.

wrong: **Emma—or "that woman" as Robert calls her, is intensely competitive.**

> *correct:*   Emma—or "that woman" as Robert calls her—is intensely compet-
> itive.

And never put a comma, a semicolon, or a colon next to a dash.

> *wrong:*   Hamlet—unlike Claudius—, is unable to act quickly and deci-
> sively.
> *correct:*   Hamlet—unlike Claudius—is unable to act quickly and decisively.

You may, however, put other punctuation marks beside parentheses. If the parenthetic element comes at the end of a sentence, put the period after the parenthesis.

> **Hamlet kills Polonius (an act that drives Ophelia to madness).**

If a whole sentence is in parentheses, the period goes inside.

> **(Berlioz lived there until April 1856.)**

Apostrophes

Apostrophes are used in three ways: to indicate possession, to mark a contraction, and to form the plural—but rarely.

- The apostrophe is used to indicate possession.

> **Atwood's handmaid narrates the story.**
> **Gentilleschi's paintings are haunting.**

You cannot use the apostrophe to indicate possession if the word is *already* in the possessive form.

> *wrong:*   The book is your's.
> *correct:*   The book is yours.

The word *yours* is a possessive pronoun. Other possessive pronouns that might cause a problem are *hers, ours, theirs,* and *its.* Never use an apostrophe with these words.

Use *'s* to make a singular noun possessive.

> **Esta's grammar is flawless.**

Even if the *singular* noun ends in *s,* make it possessive by adding *'s.*

Dickens's tone is frequently ironic.
Claudius's conscience betrays him.

Most *plural* nouns end in *s* or *es*. You make these plural nouns possessive by adding just the apostrophe.

Macbeth is reminded of the witches' prophecy.
The schools' policies have changed.

In this example, the apostrophe tells you that there are many schools.
Nouns that form the plural in another way are made possessive by adding *'s*.

Members of the women's auxiliary organized the bazaar.

To avoid errors, get straight on the plural form first. Then think about possession (whether to add just an apostrophe or *'s*).

- The apostrophe is also used to indicate a contraction (i.e., where one or more letters have been left out).

You'll never be wrong if you follow this rule.

Here, the apostrophe takes the place of the *wi* in *will*.
Don't confuse *its* (possessive form of *it*) and *it's* (contraction of *it is*).

It's unlikely that Raines will be refused permission to emigrate.

The apostrophe replaces the second *i* in *it is*.

The car has problems with its transmission.

There is no apostrophe because the word *its* is the possessive form of it.

- The apostrophe can form the plural in a few rare cases. Usually, numbers, letters, and words that are used as words are pluralized by adding only an *s*.

Joan loves music from the 1960s and 1970s.
Amina has two Ph.D.s: one in English and one in History.

Sometimes to avoid confusion, though, an apostrophe is used.

Mississippi is spelled with four s's, four i's, and two p's.

Do not make the mistake of thinking that proper nouns can be made plural by adding the apostrophe.

wrong: **The Graham's have moved to Elmira.**
correct: **The Grahams have moved to Elmira.**

VERBS

Verb Tenses

You may have some difficulty with the following:

- Present Perfect Tense

Use this tense to indicate an action or condition that began in the past and continues in the present.

The course *has been* great so far.

- Past Perfect Tense

Use this tense to indicate an action completed in the past before a specific past time (for this example, the specific past time is when you got the essay back.)

Although I *had hoped* for an A on the essay, I wasn't really surprised by the B.

- Future Perfect Tense

Use this tense to indicate an action or condition that will be completed before a specific future time.

When I finish this course, *I will have mastered* the basic principles of grammar.

- Present Progressive Tense

Use this tense for an action or condition that began in the past and is continuing in the present.

I *am writing* my rough draft.

- Past Progressive Tense

Use this tense if you want to emphasize the action or its continuing nature, or if an interruption occurs.

> I *was working* hard on my essay when Paul insisted that I try some of his tequila.

- Future Progressive Tense

Use this tense for a continuing action in the future.

> You *will be learning* about language for the rest of your life.

- Present Perfect Progressive Tense

Use this tense to emphasize the continuing nature of a single or repeated action that began in the past and has continued at least up to the present.

> I *have been working* on this paragraph for six hours.

- Past Perfect Progressive Tense

Use this tense to emphasize the continuing nature of a past action before some other past action interrupted it.

> I *had been pondering* the problem for over an hour when suddenly the solution popped into my head.

The Subjunctive Mood

When you are writing a formal essay, you will need to know about the subjunctive mood of the verb. The subjunctive mood is used to express wishes or to state a hypothetical case. The odd thing about the subjunctive mood is that in the present tense verbs do not change form to indicate the number and person of the subject but rather take the infinitive form of *be*. And in the past tense, the subjunctive takes only the plural form *were* and never the singular *was*, regardless of the subject. The subjunctive mood is found in these common expressions: *far be it from me, as it were,* and *be that as it may.*

I will provide some examples. Probably you will have heard these sentences spoken both ways; this is because in speech people often choose not to use the subjunctive. The second example gives you the sentence in the subjunctive mood so that you will know what to do in your essays.

The subjunctive is used in two main situations:

- In a clause beginning with *that* after words like *demand, recommend, urge, suggest, request, move,* and *insist.*

> I demand that my rights are acknowledged.
>
> *subjunctive:* I demand that my rights *be* acknowledged.
>
> I suggest that the committee is informed.
>
> *subjunctive:* I suggest that the committee *be* informed.

- To describe a hypothetical or very unlikely situation, a situation contrary to fact, or a wish (in an *if* or *as if* clause).

> I wish I was somewhere else.
>
> *subjunctive:* I wish I *were* somewhere else.
>
> He treats her as if she was a doll.
>
> *subjunctive:* He treats her as if she *were* a doll.

The Passive Voice

The term *voice* has to do with verbs. There are two voices: active and passive. The passive voice inverts the usual word order.

> *passive:*   The essay was written by Sinclair.
>
> *active:*   Sinclair wrote the essay.

Notice that the direct object of a sentence written in the active voice *(the essay)* becomes the subject of the sentence when it's written in the passive voice.

> *passive:*   An agreement could not be reached.
>
> *active:*   We could not reach an agreement.

Generally speaking, use the active voice. To use the passive voice is not wrong, but to overuse it weakens your writing because the passive is indirect and sometimes obscure.

Split Infinitives

In general, avoid putting something between the *to* and the base form of a verb.

> *wrong:*   She vowed to meticulously proofread her essays from now on.
>
> *correct:*   She vowed to proofread her essays meticulously from now on.

The rule against splitting the infinitive is not as firm as it once was. There are some occasions when it is acceptable to put the adverb in the middle of the infinitive, but almost always it can go either before or after the infinitive. Try out the other possibilities—see how it sounds—before deciding to break the rule.

AGREEMENT

Subject–Verb Agreement

A verb must agree with its subject in both *person* and *number*.

Agreement in Person

She walks while the others ride the bus.

She and *walks* are both third person singular; *others* and *ride* are both third person plural.

Agreement in Number

Always take the time to identify the subject of each verb. Most errors in agreement occur when the subject and verb are far apart from each other.

Here are a few cases where you might have some difficulty:

- Another noun coming between the subject and verb

A pile of papers was in the corner of the room.

The subject here is *pile* (not *papers*); it requires a singular verb *(was)*. Always be sure to identify the subject of the verb *consciously*, so that another noun in the vicinity will not mislead you!

- Compound subjects

Most compound subjects are joined by the conjunction *and*. They are easily recognizable as plural subjects.

The tenant and the landlord were at odds.

But make sure that both parts of the compound subject are indeed different things.

The architect and builder was Christopher Wren.

Here, because *architect* and *builder* refer to the same person, the verb is singular *(was)*.

His integrity and reliability make him the perfect candidate for the job.

Here, because *integrity* and *reliability* are two different things, you need the plural verb *(make)*.

Warning: Phrases like *as well as, together with* and *along with* do *not* form compound subjects and do *not* take plural verbs.

The author, together with the editor and the publicists, plans the book launch.

The subject is *author*, so you need the singular verb *(plans)*.

If a compound subject is preceded by *each* or *every*, the verb is singular.

Every character is realistic.

When a compound subject is joined by *or* or *nor*, and both parts of the subject are singular, the verb should also be singular. If both parts are plural, the verb should be plural.

Either the cord or the electrical outlet is faulty.
Neither the managers nor the workers want a prolonged strike.

Here comes the tricky case. If one half of the compound subject is plural and the other half is singular, make the verb agree with the part closest to the verb.

Because they all enjoy it so much, neither the teacher nor the students care if the class goes longer than the allotted time.

Because *students* is the part of the subject closest to the verb, you need the plural verb.

• Indefinite pronouns

Most indefinite pronouns are singular and take singular verbs. Words like *another, anybody, everyone, everything, no one, none, each, either, neither* and *someone* are singular.

Because everyone is distracted by the inspector's questions, no one notices the butler leaving the room.
None of the singers has been formally trained.

Some indefinite pronouns—words like *all, some, any* and *most*—can vary in number. They are singular if the word to which they refer is singular, and plural if the word to which they refer is plural.

All of the clothes were marked down.
All of the pie was eaten.

- Subject following the verb

Be especially careful to identify the subject if it is not in its usual position.

Wandering over the dark, foggy moor were the escaped convicts.

The subject is *convicts*, so you need the plural verb *were*.

There are several reasons why the experiment failed.

The subject here is *reasons* (not *There*—which is *never* the subject of a sentence), so the plural verb (*are*) is correct.

- The predicate noun (with linking verbs)

The predicate noun is the noun in the predicate that is linked to the subject by a linking verb, usually some form of the verb *to be*. The verb agrees with its subject, not with its predicate noun.

Sue's favourite snack is potato chips.

The subject is *snack* (not *chips*).

- Collective nouns

Collective nouns—like *faculty, audience,* and *committee*—refer to groups and may be either singular or plural. A collective noun is singular if it is considered as a whole; it is plural if it is considered in terms of its individual parts.

The committee has decided to postpone voting on this issue.

Here, the committee as a whole decided, so the noun is singular and requires a singular verb.

A number of paintings were missing.

Here, the subject is the collective noun *number*. Because the sense is plural (*paintings* clarifies this) you use the plural verb.

- Relative pronouns

To determine whether a relative pronoun *(who, which, that)* is singular or plural, identify the antecedent (the noun to which the relative pronoun refers). Then make the verb agree with the pronoun.

> **Ray's passion for computers, which serves him well on the job, drives his friends crazy.**

Here, the antecedent of the relative pronoun *which* is *passion*, a singular noun. Because *which* is singular, the verb is also singular: *serves*.

> **This is one of the best films that have ever been made.**

The subject of the dependent clause is *that*, and its antecedent is *films*; therefore *that* is plural and takes the plural verb *have*.

PRONOUNS

Pronoun Case

The case of a pronoun refers to its grammatical function within a sentence. Pronoun case varies according to how the pronoun is used.

- The object case *(him*, not *he)* is required for a pronoun that functions as the object of a verb or the object of a preposition.

> **The customs official stopped both Jane and me.**

If you remove the *Jane and* part, it's easy to see which case form you need. Many people seem to think *Jane and I* sounds better, so watch out for this one!

- Don't use the object case *(me)* or the reflexive case *(myself)* for part of a compound subject. The subject requires the subject case.

> **The engineer, the foreman, and I discussed the project in detail.**

- Use *who* or *whoever* if you need the subject case; use *whom* or *whomever* when the pronoun is the object of a verb or a preposition.

> **Professor Stanley, whom I met at the conference, is writing a book on Emily Dickinson.**

In this example, *whom* is the object of the verb *met*.

Whoever gets the job will face quite a challenge.

In this example, *whoever* is the subject of the sentence.

You should contact whoever sold you the equipment.

In this example, *whoever* is the subject of the dependent clause (which, as a whole, functions as the object of the verb *contact*).

- Comparisons using *than* or *as* can be tricky. Determine which case form is correct by completing the comparison.

Jane knows more about literary theory than I.

If you complete the comparison (". . . than I know"), it's easy to see which case form you need.

Pronoun Agreement

Pronouns must agree with their antecedents in *gender* and in *number*.

Agreement in Gender

It is no longer acceptable to use the third person masculine pronoun *(he)* when the gender of a noun is unspecified.

wrong: **A doctor should carefully monitor his patient's recovery.**

Do not avoid the issue of gender by switching to the plural pronoun.

wrong: **A doctor should carefully monitor their patient's recovery.**

This produces an error in number: *doctor* is singular; *their* is plural.
There are several ways of handling this problem:

- Change everything to the plural.

correct: **Doctors should carefully monitor their patients' recovery.**

- Use a gender-inclusive construction.

correct: A doctor should carefully monitor his or her patient's recovery.

- Rewrite the sentence to avoid using a pronoun.

correct: A patient's recovery should be carefully monitored.
correct: Doctors should carefully monitor the recovery of patients.

Agreement in Number

- When two nouns are joined by *or* or *nor*, the pronoun (like the verb) agrees with the noun that is closest to it.

Neither the minister nor his aides seem confident of their answers.

- Watch out for prepositional phrases that follow the subject. Be sure you've got the right antecedent for the pronoun.

The circle of stones at Stonehenge continues to conceal its true function.

The antecedent of *its* is *circle*, not *stones*.

- Remember that collective nouns can be singular or plural according to context.

The jazz ensemble cancelled its concert tour.

- Most indefinite pronouns (words like *everyone*) are singular; but some (words like *any* or *some*) are variable. They are either singular or plural, according to the number of the noun to which they refer.

Some of the wine is gone.
Some of the photographs have lost their colour.

- The number of a relative pronoun *(who, which, that)* depends on the number of its antecedent.

In the drawer was a collection of butterfly specimens, which had retained their colour despite their age.

The antecedent of *which* is *specimens*, so the plural pronoun *(their)* is required.

Pronoun Reference

A pronoun must clearly refer to only one noun. An *ambiguous* pronoun reference results when more than one noun could be the antecedent of the pronoun.

> *ambiguous:* **When Carolyn met Lynn, she was pregnant.**

The pronoun *she* could refer to either Carolyn or Lynn.

> *correct:* **When she met Lynn, Carolyn was pregnant.**
> *correct:* **Carolyn was pregnant when she met Lynn.**

A broad pronoun reference error means that there is no single noun in the sentence that could be the antecedent of the pronoun.

> *broad:* **The NDP candidate was ahead in the polls, but, in the end, they didn't vote for him.**

There is no noun to serve as the antecedent of *they.*

> *correct:* **The NDP candidate was ahead in the polls, but, in the end, the voters didn't elect him.**

PARALLEL CONSTRUCTION AND PLACEMENT

Parallel construction and the correct placement of modifiers are important for the clarity in your prose: if either is faulty, the meaning of your sentence may be obscured.

Parallelism

Parallelism means that one part of the sentence is parallel (similar in form) to another part.

> **The professor warned her class *that plagiarism* is a crime and *that a student* caught plagiarizing would be punished.**

Here, two noun clauses *(that plagiarism . . . and that a student . . .)* are parallel.

You can avoid faulty parallelism by paying attention to these rules:

- Coordinate conjunctions join like things.

wrong:	Offred likes *playing* Scrabble and *to read* magazines with the Commander.
correct:	Offred likes *playing* Scrabble and *reading* magazines with the Commander.

- Parallel elements are required after correlative conjunctions. Correlative conjunctions always come in pairs: *both . . . and, not . . . but, either . . . or, neither . . . nor, not only . . . but also.*

wrong:	Some would say that because he leaves them both, Shabine neither *loves his wife* nor *his mistress.*
correct:	Some would say that because he leaves them both, Shabine loves neither *his wife* nor *his mistress.*

Note that the position of the verb *(loves)* in the first sentence destroys the parallel structure.

- Elements in a series must be parallel in form.

wrong:	The novel is intriguing, suspenseful, and introduces some weird characters.
correct:	The novel is intriguing and suspenseful and introduces some weird characters.

Note that the first sentence sets up a false series because the elements are not similar in form (not all adjectives). In the second sentence, the faulty parallelism has been corrected by using another conjunction.

- Omission sometimes produces faulty parallelism.

wrong:	Jimmy Sr. never has and never will complain about his position in the van.
correct:	Jimmy Sr. never has complained and never will complain about his position in the van.

Don't forget part of the verb. The insertion of *complained* is necessary because you can't say "never has complain."

- Comparisons require you to compare like things.

wrong:	His muscles are as big as a weight lifter.
correct:	His muscles are as big as a weight lifter's [muscles].

If you complete the comparison in your head, you'll see which form is correct.

Placement of Modifiers

Place a modifier as close as possible to the thing it modifies.

Compare these sentences and notice how the meaning changes when the modifier *only* is moved.

Only my friend eats vegetables.
My only friend eats vegetables.
My friend only eats vegetables. (He doesn't *wear* them, for example.)
My friend eats only vegetables.

A shift in placement will not always produce a shift in meaning, but it may produce confusion.

A *squinting modifier* is particularly confusing. This error occurs when a modifier is placed between two things, either of which it could logically modify.

squinting:　**The tenor said in the evening he would sing at the concert.**

The prepositional phrase *in the evening* could modify *said*, telling you when the tenor made the announcement; or it could modify *sing*, telling you when he would sing. Take the modifier out of the middle.

correct:　**The tenor said he would sing at the concert in the evening.**

Dangling Modifiers

A *dangling modifier* is a modifier that doesn't have anything to modify or seems to modify the wrong thing.

A common type of dangling modifier is the dangling participle. The rule is that the nearest noun or pronoun must be the actor of the verb in the participle.

wrong:　**Turning the pages, the images seemed to come alive before my eyes.**

The phrase *Turning the pages* hooks onto the first noun and modifies it. Here, the first noun is *images*—and that's obviously wrong.

correct:　**Turning the pages, I saw the images come alive before my eyes.**
correct:　**As I turned the pages, the images seemed to come alive before my eyes.**

Here are several other examples of dangling modifiers.

wrong: **By examining the facts, a conclusion can be reached.**

The *conclusion* cannot *examine the facts.*

correct: **By examining the facts, we can reach a conclusion.**
wrong: **To understand the meaning clearly, the poem must be read aloud.**

This is a dangling infinitive phrase. The *poem* does not *understand.*

correct: **To understand the meaning clearly, we must read the poem aloud.**
wrong: **Once in university, students' work habits have to change.**

This is a dangling elliptical clause where the subject and verb (once *they are* in university) are only understood. The *students' work habits* are not *in university;* the students are. The problem is that once it has been made possessive, *students'* functions as an adjective rather than a noun.

correct: **Once they are in university, students must change their work habits.**
wrong: **A timeless theme, the poem is entirely about love.**

This is a dangling appositive. The *poem* is not a *timeless theme.*

correct: A timeless theme, love is the poem's subject.

To show you the kinds of placement errors that are often made, I have come up with a paragraph that contains dangling and misplaced modifiers. See if you can find them.

By writing what is considered to be a quintessentially modernist piece, we can see that T.S. Eliot, in his poem "The Love Song of J. Alfred Prufrock," demonstrates the fragmentation of the modern self. Prufrock issues an invitation—"Let us go then, you and I"—but the "you" more than likely refers to a part of his own psyche, at the beginning of the poem. Worried at the party about how others see him, Prufrock feels "formulated, sprawling on a pin." Wondering whether he dares to "disturb the universe," and deciding that it is ultimately not worth the effort, the poem expresses the insecurity of Prufrock.

Now let's compare notes. In the first sentence, it sounds as though *we* wrote the poem when, in fact, *Eliot* did. The error in the second sentence is perhaps more subtle; here the phrase "at the beginning of the poem" is misplaced, since it refers to the word "you" and not to the state of Prufrock's psyche. Do you see the difference? In the next sentence, the placement of the prepositional phrase "at the party" is confusing, since it seems to suggest that Prufrock is anxious only at the party (and not at other times). But the phrase is meant to modify others (others at the party). Remember to put the modifier as close as possible to what it modifies. In the final sentence there is another example of a dangling modifier: it is not the *poem* that is wondering and deciding, but rather Prufrock himself.

Now I'll rewrite the whole paragraph, and clear up all those placement errors.

By writing what is considered to be a quintessentially modernist piece—"The Love Song of J. Alfred Prufrock"—T.S. Eliot demonstrates the fragmentation of the modern self. At the beginning of the poem, Prufrock issues an invitation—"Let us go then, you and I"—but the "you" more than likely refers to a part of his own psyche rather than to another person. He is worried about how others at the party see him, and claims that he feels "formulated, sprawling on a pin." By wondering whether he dares to "disturb the universe," and by deciding that it is ultimately not worth the effort, Prufrock reveals his insecurity.

Do you see how much easier this is to read? The correct placement of modifiers will make your prose *much* clearer.

Mixed Constructions

When writing longer, more complex sentences, don't lose track of a construction you've begun.

wrong: **The thought of borrowing a large sum of money is so intimidating and takes so long to pay back that many young couples choose to rent rather than buy.**

The problem here is that the writer has forgotten the subject of the sentence, and has treated *a large sum of money* as the subject of *takes* when it isn't. The sentence begins with the subject—*thought*—which cannot be the subject of *takes*.

correct: **The thought of borrowing a large sum of money and of having to pay it back for so long causes many young couples to rent rather than to buy.**

Incomplete Constructions

Always remember to complete a construction that you set up.

wrong: **As far as racism, many people believe it simply isn't a problem in Canada.**

This phrase must be completed: "As far as racism is concerned . . ."

correct: **As far as racism is concerned, many people believe it simply isn't a problem in Canada.**

correct: **As for racism, many people believe it simply isn't a problem in Canada.**

GLOSSARY OF USAGE

accept, except

Accept is a verb meaning receive or approve of; *except* means exclude or with the exception of.

> *example:* Except for Jason, we all *accepted* the proposal.

affect, effect

Affect is a verb meaning to act upon or to influence; *effect* is a noun meaning result or consequence.

> *example:* The medication had no immediate effect.
> *example:* The partial loss of his hearing *affected* Paul's performance.

Effect can also be used as a verb, meaning to bring about or to cause, but this use is not common.

> *example:* The Prime Minister promised to *effect* significant changes to the tax laws during his term in office.

allude, refer

When you *allude* to something you make indirect reference to it, while to *refer* to something is to make direct reference.

> *example:* His use of the white mask alludes to *The Phantom of the Opera*.
> *example:* In my essay I *refer* extensively to the work of Walter Jackson Bate.

allusion, illusion

An *allusion* is a brief, indirect reference to a person, event, or literary work. An *illusion* is a magical or misleading appearance.

example: There is an allusion to *Hamlet* in T.S. Eliot's poem "The Love Song of J. Alfred Prufrock."

example: Wearing vertical stripes gives the *illusion* of being tall and thin.

amount, number

Use *number* when referring to something you can count, and *amount* when referring to a mass or total.

> *wrong:* I was amazed at the *amount* of people at the recital.
>
> *correct:* I was amazed at the *number* of people at the recital.
>
> *example:* The dentist was alarmed at the *amount* of tooth decay.

complement, compliment (complementary, complimentary)

Complementary indicates a completion or a fitting together of parts. *Complimentary* is an adjective indicating praise; it also means *free*, as in a complimentary cup of coffee.

> *example:* The style and the content *complement* each other in Ishiguro's novel *The Remains of the Day.*
>
> *example:* Indira always receives lots of *compliments* when she sings.

conscious, conscience

Conscious is an adjective meaning aware or awake, whereas *conscience* means the part of you that dictates your moral code of behaviour. *Conscientious* means scrupulous or upright.

> *example:* I was *conscious* of the student's uneasiness as she wrote the exam.
>
> *example:* Lady Macbeth was destroyed by her guilty *conscience.*

denotation, connotation.

The *denotation* of a word is its literal, dictionary definition. *Connotation* refers to all of the associations that you make when you see or hear that word.

> *example:* A beach *denotes* a stretch of sand at the edge of a body of water, but it *connotes* a place to build sand castles or go swimming.

disinterested, uninterested

To be *disinterested* means to be objective or neutral, while to be *uninterested* indicates boredom.

> *example:* Because they were a *disinterested* group of individuals, the jury made a fair decision.

> *example:* They showed they were *uninterested* by rolling their eyes and watching the clock.

explicit, implicit

If something is expressed *explicitly* it is expressed directly or spelled out very clearly. To express something *implicitly* is to imply it or to express it indirectly.

> *example:* I left *explicit* instructions about how to take care of the dog.
> *example:* *Implicitly*, the poet is talking about death.

infer, imply

These two words do not mean the same thing. *Imply* means to suggest or hint at; *infer* means to conclude by reasoning, to deduce.

> *example:* The police officer *inferred* from her calm demeanour that she hadn't seen anything important.
> *example:* Without saying so, she strongly *implied* that the jewels were fake.

is when, is where

Both of these expressions are incorrect. Adverb clauses that begin with *when* or *where* cannot follow the linking verb *is*.

> *wrong:* In Bridge, a grand slam *is when* one team wins all the tricks.
> *correct:* In Bridge, a grand slam occurs when one team wins all the tricks.

its, it's

Its is a possessive pronoun, while *it's* is a contraction of either *it is* or *it has*.

> *example:* Clark Blaise says that a story is *its* beginning amplified.
> *example:* *It's* unusual for my sister to read anything but mystery novels.

less, fewer

Use *less* in comparisons when the things compared can't be counted and *fewer* when they can be counted.

> *example:* The old man has *fewer* teeth than his wife.
> *example:* At this moment, I have *less* self-confidence than I did at twenty.

lie, lay, lain, lying, laid

To lay is a verb that means to put or place. It always takes an object.

> *example:* I *lay* the baby on the bed.

I am *laying* the baby on the bed.
I *laid* the baby on the bed.
I have *laid* the baby on the bed.

Lie is a verb meaning to recline; it does *not* take an object. But note that the past tense of *lie* is *lay.*

> *example:* I *lie* on the floor.
> I *lay* on the floor.
> I have *lain* on the floor.
> I am *lying* on the floor.

like, as

Learn how to use these words. They are not interchangeable. Remember that *like* is a preposition (it takes a noun object; it does *not* introduce a clause), and *as* is a conjunction (it *can* introduce a clause).

> *wrong:* Rover stood stiffly alert, pointing, head and tail down, as any well-
> trained dog.
> (Should be *like* because it is followed by a noun and its modifiers, not a clause.)

> *wrong:* Roger is dressed exactly like Ray is.
> (Should be *as* because it is followed by a clause.)

lose, loose

Loose is an adjective that means not tight, or a verb meaning to release (often *loosen*). *To lose* is a verb, the opposite of to win or to find.

> *example:* The child was excited because her first tooth was *loose.*
> *example:* You might want to *loosen* your tie since it's so hot in here.
> *example*: Sophie hates to *lose* at tennis.

practice, practise

Practice is a noun; *practise* is a verb.

> *example:* In the seventeenth century, many women were accused of *practising*
> witchcraft.
> *example:* Gretzky always attended hockey *practice.*

principal, principle

Principal is an adjective meaning primary or main (or a noun meaning the head of a school); *principle* is a noun meaning fundamental truth.

example: The *principal* reason for the product's success is good advertising.
example: Today we learned about the *principles* of thermodynamics.

quote, quotation

To *quote* is a verb; *quotation* is a noun. (Do *not* say "this quote . . .")

example: It isn't necessary to quote the entire passage.
example: The quotation comes from Milton's *Paradise Lost.*

who, that

Both *who* and *that* are relative pronouns. Generally *who* refers to people and *that* refers to things. Sometimes, however, *that* can refer to people, especially to groups or classes of people.

example: It was John *who* called last night.
example: I used the same travel agent *that* Jungwei did.
example: The media literacy committee *that* meets on Thursdays is organizing a conference.

Note: Often *that* is used to eliminate the awkwardness of using whom.

example: A woman *that* I knew years ago moved in next door.

that, which

That and *which* are relative pronouns that generally refer to things—but they are not interchangeable! *Which* begins *nonrestrictive* clauses; *that* begins *restrictive* clauses.

example: I am most proud of the essay *that* I wrote last semester. (restrictive)
example: Peter's new digital alarm clock, *which* he bought at Canadian Tire, came with a warranty. (nonrestrictive)

who, whom

Who is a pronoun that is used as a subject, while *whom* is the object form of the pronoun.

example: *Who* is the heroine of *Pride and Prejudice*?
example: The author, of *whom* you spoke so highly, is giving a reading tomorrow night.

verbal, oral

These words do not mean the same thing. *Verbal* means pertaining to words; *oral* means spoken aloud.